UNWRITTEN MEMORIES

Katia Mann
UNWRITTEN
MEMORIES

EDITED BY
ELISABETH PLESSEN
AND MICHAEL MANN
TRANSLATED FROM THE
GERMAN BY HUNTER AND
HILDEGARDE HANNUM

New York:
Alfred · A · Knopf
1975

AAL 9919

Editors' Note

KATIA MANN'S EPIGRAPH explains just about everything concerning these "unwritten memories" except the manner in which they were finally turned into a written document.

Until Elisabeth Plessen ultimately succeeded in gaining interviews with the narrator, Katia Mann had resisted being coaxed into telling her life story. When she finally agreed, she spoke for many hours. Some of the material appeared as television programs; the rest of her narration was reshaped chronologically.

Most of these reminiscences remained in a half-finished state for several years, in keeping with Katia Mann's wishes. Then, in the summer of 1973, when she reached her ninetieth birthday, this fragmentary material came into the hands of her son, Michael Mann. During a relaxed meeting between the two in the Engadine, her story underwent further revision. Every day he had to think of new ways to arouse her interest in the manuscript: on the terrace at teatime, for instance, after casually asking her some specific question or other having to do with a passage in the text, he solicitously supplied her with reading glasses and pencil

—and the battle was won! Then Katia Mann would often sit working over the manuscript until dinner time, shaking her head, making eager use of the glasses and pencil, and not infrequently concluding, "This is really an amusing story after all!"

A number of possibly unfamiliar persons appear in this history; some information about them is available in alphabetical order at the back of the book. The narration has occasionally been interrupted by "interjections from outside." The intermingled voices—deriving from the original form of these memoirs—are identified as G.M. (Golo Mann), E.M. (Erika Mann), and, obviously, K.M. (Katia Mann).

ELISABETH PLESSEN,
MICHAEL MANN, 1974

ILLUSTRATIONS

(following page 86)

*The photographs in this volume, with few exceptions,
have been supplied by the Thomas Mann Archiv
and members of the Mann family.*

Katia, April 1886. J. C. SCHAARWÄCHTER, BERLIN.

Katia and her twin brother, Klaus Pringsheim, April 1885.
J. C. SCHAARWÄCHTER, BERLIN.

The five Pringsheim children: Peter, Heinz, Klaus, Erik, and
Katia, April 1886. J. C. SCHAARWÄCHTER, BERLIN.

Children's Carnival: Four Pierrots and a Pierrette, the
Pringsheim children, 1889. OIL PAINTING BY FRIEDRICH
AUGUST VON KAULBACH.

Hedwig Pringsheim and her children, Arcistrasse, Munich,
1891: Peter, Erik, Klaus, Katia, and Heinz.

Katia with her mother, 1889–90.

Katia, April 1887. J. C. SCHAARWÄCHTER, BERLIN.

Katia, 1893. GEBR. LÜTZEL, MUNICH.

Katia, 1899. OIL PAINTING BY FRIEDRICH AUGUST VON
KAULBACH.

Katia, 1892. OIL PAINTING BY FRANZ VON LENBACH.

Klaus and Katia, ready to enter university, 1900.
JAEGER & GOERGEN, MUNICH.

Katia with her son Klaus on the veranda. Arcistrasse,
Munich, 1907.

Illustrations

❀◇❀◇❀◇❀◇❀◇❀◇❀◇❀◇❀◇❀◇❀◇❀

Katia and her children at their home in Munich, September
1919: Erika, Elisabeth, Klaus, Katia, Michael, Golo,
and Monika.

Katia with Erika and Klaus, 1907.

Katia with Golo in her arms, Erika, Thomas, and Klaus,
Tölz, 1909.

On Alfred Pringsheim's eightieth birthday at the Manns'
vacation home, Nidden, September 2, 1930: Elisabeth,
Golo, Katia, Alfred and Hedwig Pringsheim, and
Thomas. FRITZ KRAUSKOPF, KÖNIGSBERG.

Katia, Elisabeth, and Arthur Nikisch (son of the famous
conductor), Arosa, Winter 1933.

Thomas and Katia, Nidden, Summer 1930.

Golo, Mrs. René Schickele, Mrs. Julius Meier-Graefe,
Thomas, Julius Meier-Graefe, Katia, her cousin Ilse
Dernberg, and Erika, Sanary, 1933.

Katia and her son Klaus, 1927. E. WASOW, MUNICH.

Thomas and Katia, New York, April 1937.
ALFRED A. KNOPF.

Else and Bruno Walter with Katia, Pacific Palisades,
1943.

Katia and Thomas with their grandsons Frido and Tonio,
Pacific Palisades, 1948. FLORENCE HOMOLKA.

Thomas Mann's seventy-fifth birthday, Zurich, June 6,
1950: Gret (Mrs. Michael Mann), Thomas, Katia, Erika,
Elisabeth, and Michael. HEINZ GUGGENBÜHL.

Katia with Frido and Tonio, Erlenbach, 1953.
ELLEN ERBY.

Thomas and Katia in their garden, Kilchberg-Zurich, 1955.
FRITZ ESCHEN, BERLIN.

Katia, Zurich, 1966. HERTHA RAMME, ZURICH.

Katia in her garden, Kilchberg-Zurich, 1971.
ⓒ STUDIO BLIGGI, ZURICH.

ACTUALLY, I have always kept my whole, all too long life strictly private. I never called attention to myself; I didn't think it appropriate.

People are always saying I should write my memoirs. My answer is that there must be one person in this family who doesn't write.

The fact that I am now letting myself in for these interviews can only be attributed to my weakness and good nature.

KATIA MANN, 1970

UNWRITTEN MEMORIES

I

M Y FATHER was a professor of mathematics at the University of Munich, my mother was a beautiful woman, and I was a completely unexpected addition to the family. My parents were staying on the Starnberger See for the summer with my three older brothers. They had rented a little house there in Feldafing. My father went in to Munich two or three times a week for his classes—he was a Privatdozent at the university.

My mother was expecting her fourth child, and when it came, and came too early, there were two: my twin brother and, quite unexpectedly, myself! No one was in attendance except a peasant woman, and there was no telephone. The midwife said, "Jessas! There's another one coming!" And there I was.

When my father came home that day, he was welcomed excitedly: "Herr Doktor! Herr Doktor! It's twins!" He almost had a stroke.

That was the beginning, and then I grew up. At first, my twin brother, Klaus, and I were naturally very close, since we always did everything together. We had private lessons at home for the first three years of schooling. I don't know why. Perhaps because I was rather

delicate, we weren't supposed to go to the Volksschule *
as ordinary children did. Every day a teacher, a Herr
Schülein, tutored us for one hour. From him my twin
brother and I received our entire elementary education.
Then Klaus took the entrance examination for the Gymnasium,† and I was all alone. It was my mother's idea
(and also my grandmother's) that I should have a Gymnasium education. At that time there was no Gymnasium
for girls in Munich, and of course no coeducational
schools as there are today; consequently, various Gymnasium professors took turns giving me private instruc-
tion. First, a student who came to the house to supervise
my four brothers in their lessons tutored me in the
courses required up to the third form—I found them a
mere trifle. After that, Gymnasium teachers came, each
staying for about two hours a week: one for classical
languages, one for mathematics, and one for German
and history. The material was terribly easy for me to
learn: when you are alone, you learn rapidly. In school
you always have to adjust yourself to the average or below average, and I was above average. During the last
year, I was tutored by a professor of religion from the
Gymnasium, a Dr. Engelhardt. I read the New Testa-
ment with him in Greek (religion was a requirement at
the Gymnasium).

Once, I remember, we came to the story in which
Jesus meets the woman of Samaria and says to her: "You

* Volksschule corresponds to elementary or primary school in
Great Britain and the United States.
† A Gymnasium is a secondary school in German-speaking
countries that prepares students for the university.

have had five husbands, and the man you are living with now is not your husband." Here the teacher became embarrassed; his comment was: "That's the situation among the lower classes."

And so it went until I was sixteen. Then, as a special student, I took the Abitur * with my twin brother at the Wilhelms-Gymnasium, and it went splendidly. Now I was supposed to go to the university. I specialized in the natural sciences: experimental physics with Wilhelm Röntgen and mathematics with my father—calculus and the theory of functions. But I have always felt that I had no special aptitude for these subjects. One of my brothers, Peter, the second eldest, also studied physics and became a very good physicist. I wasn't predestined for that at all, and Röntgen didn't think much of me either. Once during an experiment I had a minor disaster: I knocked over an apparatus. Röntgen took that rather badly. Probably I would never have excelled in his subject, nor did I find myself very talented in mathematics. I took those courses because of filial attachment, and I've forgotten them all.

Maybe I would have completed my studies and taken my degree. However, I had studied for only four or six semesters when I got married; soon after that the first baby arrived, and the second one right away, and very soon the third and fourth. That was the end of my studies.

. . .

---

* The Abitur is a qualifying examination for study at a university.

My parents kept quite a fine house, as the saying goes. Their home was highly regarded and much visited, and they gave large parties. As a result of my father's profession and his personal inclinations it was an academic household with musical interests. In contrast to my mother, he did not have a very lively interest in literature. Many people came to Arcistrasse, some writers among them, although the majority were musicians and painters. Richard Strauss visited us, as did the Schillings, Fritz August von Kaulbach, Franz von Lenbach, Franz von Stuck, and many others from Munich's social and artistic circles.

My father, an early Wagner enthusiast, had persuaded his parents to buy share certificates—patronage certificates they were called—for the construction of the theater in Bayreuth. He knew Wagner personally, and one or two letters Wagner had written him were among his sacred possessions. In 1876 he was in Bayreuth for the rehearsals of the *Ring*, but he was never an intimate visitor at Wagner's home, Wahnfried; because he had once fought a duel in Bayreuth on Wagner's account, he had forfeited his personal relationship with the people at Wahnfried. At a restaurant, someone nearby had spoken disparagingly about Wagner, and my father, who had a quick temper, hit the man on the head with a beer glass. He was thereafter called the "Schoppenhauer." * The man challenged him, and a duel

---

* A Schoppen is a pint-sized glass for beer or wine; a "Schoppenhauer"—a pun of course on the name of the famous philosopher—is someone who hits out with one of these glasses.

with pistols ensued without any blood being spilled. They were terribly annoyed about the whole thing at Wahnfried. They didn't want any scandal. My father nevertheless remained a passionate Wagnerite for the rest of his life. He adapted many Wagner pieces for piano, for four hands as well as for two, and these arrangements were played in our home. We had a very pretty music room, in which there was a good deal of musicmaking. Stars from the opera came often. An outstanding Wagner singer, a prima donna called Ternina for whom my father had the very highest regard, often sang for us.

When I was eleven, I went to the *Meistersinger* for the first time. "Ah, the child will fall asleep," everyone said. Instead, I was sorry when it was over. Indeed, I grew up with Wagnerian music; from childhood I had the idea that Wagner's works were the most marvelous thing on earth.

In those days Munich was a city of art; it was less of a literary city, and writers didn't count for much. Thus, whenever my husband went into a store, he was addressed as "Herr Kunstmaler" (painter). I can't really say that I had any early training for a life with writers. Of course I knew several of them even as a child, but none of them made much of an impression on me.

The first writer I knew was my grandmother Hedwig Dohm, the wife of Ernst Dohm, who founded *Kladderadatsch* (a humorous periodical). She wrote novels which probably would not have much appeal for the reader of today. I couldn't say how old I was when I first read something by her. One of her books was called *Women's Nature and Rights*. She was a passionate early champion of women, who really did not have many rights yet. As I've already mentioned, there wasn't even a Gymnasium for girls at that time. My grandmother dearly loved her eldest, most gifted, and most beautiful daughter, my mother, and they wrote to each other, I believe, at least two or three times a week. My mother wrote long reports from Munich to Berlin, and my grandmother saved them all. She then incorporated everything in the letters about Munich society into her novel *Sibilla Dalmar,* and that caused a veritable scandal —all the more since the figure in the book corresponding to my mother had an affair with a Baltic nobleman, which in reality was not the case. This was particularly annoying for my father. My grandmother, however, a naïve and at the same time gifted woman, had had no second thoughts about the matter at all.

She later became, at least for me, a regular figure out of a fairy tale. She was small, and she kept getting smaller. Lenbach painted a lovely portrait of her, which we still have. She had a fine head, and all her grandchildren were devoted to her. We went to Merano together, my husband and I, with "Urmiemchen," my children's name for her. On the train Urmiemchen said, "Oh, Tommy, Tommy! Quick! Please come to my compartment and help me. Everything in the sleeping car is made for giants."

She was very little, very quaint, and, in her way, a delightful old lady.

Annette Kolb was a friend from the time I was eleven. She was a regular guest in our home—she was already writing then—and I always used the familiar "du" with her.

Paul Heyse was also a regular guest of ours, and he couldn't believe that I had never read anything by him; he was very disappointed. At that time I was around fourteen. He visited my mother, and she said, "I must introduce you to my daughter, Katia." Whereupon he said, assuming that I must have read him, "Well, you have, haven't you . . . ?" I said, "Yes, I think so. . . ." He had such a gentle voice and a soft little beard and beautiful blue eyes, and was so vain.

I met Max Halbe, Wolfskehl, Countess Reventlow. But I didn't know any of them well.

My father was not much in favor of my marrying a writer. He always said, "A writer isn't quite the thing, don't you agree? It's rather on the frivolous side." He thought it had to be a young scholar, a university professor (and at that time I even had a suitor who was a professor). My mother was in favor of my marrying Thomas Mann; she was agreeable to it from the first. My father wasn't, to the same extent, but he didn't try to prevent the marriage. He wouldn't have been able to anyway. One of the additional reasons that he didn't like the idea was that as the only daughter in a family with four boys, I was a little ray of sunshine, wasn't I? I shouldn't leave home so soon. He just didn't like it; that's the way fathers are. Thomas Mann described this to some degree in *Royal Highness*. I now think I must have been quite pretty as a girl, but the sad part about it is that I wasn't aware of it then at all. No one in my family ever had the kindness to inform me. Since my mother was a celebrated beauty and one of my grand-mothers (my father's mother) said to me whenever she saw me, "Ah, you'll never be the equal of your mother!" I accepted that idea. A shame, really. Else Lasker-Schüler once described me to someone as an Oriental princess; I consider that very exaggerated.

Naturally, many suitors appeared. Many young people were regular guests at our house; they all more or less paid court to me, and one or the other would certainly have liked to marry me. But I didn't give marriage a thought, not even when I met Thomas Mann and he showed interest in me. I didn't take it very seri-ously, and it would never have occurred to me to marry him. Marriage was his idea.

A young man from Silesia, whose name was Prings-heim, like my own, was a frequent guest at our house. Apparently he was very much in love with me. Perhaps he was distantly related to us, but that was impossible to prove. He was an especially serious student and good-looking as well. We attended the university together and always went there on our bicycles when the weather permitted, leaving them in the so-called bike stall. When classes were over, we went back to get them. I can recall that once I went unsuspectingly to get my bike, and there the young man with my name appeared and declared his affection, which amounted to a proposal of marriage—right there in the bike stall. I was com-pletely "flabbergasted," as the Americans say, com-pletely speechless, and kept saying, "But why in the world? Whatever gave you that idea? I'll have to think it over—I mean, this is much too sudden. I wasn't thinking of any such thing just now. I mean, I like you very much, but I never thought of marrying you. We can wait a while. . . ." and so on. He was rather nonplussed and went off.

Later I offended him again by mistake. On Sundays we always had a lot of young people for tea, and he was there too. We were talking about how funny it is that girls quite suddenly have a different name when they marry, which is not the case with men. I said I was now in the fortunate position of not having to change my name at all, and laughed. After that he wrote me an eight-page letter, saying that it had been dreadful for him, and I should never again make jokes about things which were sacred to him. He would never get over it. I hadn't meant any harm, but nevertheless I apologized profusely.

That was one of my suitors. I had others as well, but they were all very young and insignificant. It occurs to me that Alfred Kerr had also wanted to marry me, but I never shared his intention. For the rest of his life he held this against Thomas Mann, quite apart from his other nastiness toward him. I didn't marry any of them, not the professor or the greatly offended Pringsheim, or Kerr, or the others, but—after some delays on my part —Thomas Mann.

We got to know each other in a very funny way. Thomas Mann "knew" me from a childhood portrait, but without knowing that his future wife was portrayed on the canvas. It was quite strange. When my brothers and I were children—we were very close in age, only four years between the oldest and youngest—the five of us once went to a children's masquerade ball in Munich, the four boys dressed as Pierrots and I as Pierrette. We wore white costumes with black pompoms, long black stockings, and tall white hats. The boys wore wide pants and I a short skirt. Also at the ball was the painter Fritz August von Kaulbach, who was very much in vogue in Munich at that time as indeed he was in all Germany. He was portrait painter to the court and, next to Lenbach, the ranking painter of the day. Kaulbach was a friend of the family giving the ball and also knew my parents, and when he saw us five children that evening, he was utterly captivated by the five Pierrots. He then visited my parents, telling them that he had seen us at the ball and that we had been such a delightful sight that he simply had to paint us in our costumes. Well, he painted the five of us, and the picture was a colossal success, as genre paintings were at that time. The Pierrot picture was then exhibited in many German cities and appeared in various magazines. Friends of ours who had been to St. Petersburg even brought back paper napkins with this picture as a decoration in one corner. The young Thomas, who was fourteen years old at the time the picture was done (I was six), was still living in Lübeck and, like so many others, saw the picture in a magazine. He liked it so much that he cut it out and tacked it up over his desk. Thus he always had it before his eyes, but had no idea who these children were, for the name of the family of course didn't appear; the picture was simply called *Children's Carnival*. He told me this later. The painting hung in our living room, and when he was a guest in our house, he naturally saw it and realized that I was one of the children. But at what point he became aware of this connection, I really couldn't say. I don't know whether his interest in me had anything to do with the picture he had had as a boy. I never asked him about it. His interest was more likely directed toward me as I was at twenty when he saw me in Munich. He had already been observing me at a distance and from "above," before we met face to face.

Whenever I went out, I was always surrounded by my four brothers. I never appeared by myself, for in those days a young girl wasn't allowed on the street alone. We went to many parties and attended many concerts together. Along with the already existing Akademie concerts at the Odeon, there was a newly formed concert enterprise in Munich, the so-called Kaim concerts, which, along with the Odeon concerts, were supposed to enrich the city's musical life. The entrepreneur was a man named Kaim. He had founded an orchestra and built a concert hall, Kaim Hall, but had miscalculated the building expenses and was close to bankruptcy; so the music lovers of Munich were being strongly urged to take out subscriptions in order to support this second concert series. My father also had a subscription. He had bought five subscriptions right off, and I always went with my four brothers. Felix Weingartner was the conductor. My husband-to-be, who was very musical and always a great lover of music and who also attended these concerts regularly, saw me there with my brothers, observed the family from above, especially the girl, and liked what he saw. So he had known me by sight for a long time. But I didn't know him, although I had read *Buddenbrooks* by then.

My parents were of course well known in Munich, and these five children who always appeared together were conspicuous and well known too. I can recall that once, during an intermission at one of these concerts, a Bavarian prince, Prince Luitpold, spoke to me, asking, "Aren't you Fräulein Pringsheim?" and so on. He was very gracious and I very embarrassed; I replied nervously, "It's probably going to start again now," and withdrew. Someone called after me, "What about the court curtsey?" But I had no idea how to make a court curtsey. After all, I had hardly ever spoken with princes. I wonder whether my husband had also observed this princely rencontre, since he was always watching me.

After we were married, my four brothers continued to appear in closed ranks. I recall that Hofmannsthal, who often came to Munich, said to someone when he was at a concert and saw my brothers, "How nice, Katia's brothers! They're always talking to one another." We knew him quite well, and I was on cordial terms with him. To be sure, I was never in Rodaun (a suburb of Vienna where Hofmannsthal made his home), but my husband was, and he was greatly taken with it. He got along very well with Hofmannsthal, had a very high opinion of him as a writer, and always esteemed him as a human being. Hofmannsthal's death affected him deeply.

But back to the years 1903 and 1904. I didn't meet Thomas Mann until after the episode in the streetcar. When not using my bicycle, I always went to classes by streetcar in the morning and again in the afternoon, and Thomas Mann often took the same car. I had to get out at the stop at the corner of Schelling and Türkenstrasse and walk the rest of the way, with my briefcase under my arm. Once, as I was about to get off, the conductor came up and said, "Your ticket."

I: "I'm getting off here."

He: "I have to have your ticket."

I: "But I'm telling you that I'm getting off. I've just thrown it away because I'm getting off here."

He: "I have to have the ticket. Your ticket, I said."

"Just leave me alone," I said, and jumped off in a rage.

He called after me, "Get going, you little devil!"

This delighted my future husband so much that he said to himself: "I have always wanted to meet her; this settles it."

But where? We had many friends and acquaintances in common in Munich, and he could have gone to several of them with the request to invite him along with me and to seat us next to each other. At the Stucks', for example, we could have met quite easily. Franz von Stuck, actually of peasant descent, a very successful painter with his symbolic pictures—later he was even ennobled—had built a beautiful house in Roman style

which he designed himself, the Villa Stuck. He also designed the furnishings for it. Frau von Stuck was a very
beautiful woman. In this villa they gave large parties,
and since she had unusual views on the seating of guests,
it would have been easy for Thomas Mann to get to
know me there. We would automatically have found
ourselves at the same table, perhaps even next to each
other. The Stucks used the following plan for seating
their guests: they put all the aristocrats at one table; at
the second they put all the "better" people, including
my parents and me—and Thomas Mann sat there when
he was a guest—and at the third table they seated the
leftovers, people they felt they couldn't inflict on anyone. It really wasn't a very good method of division.

Thomas Mann thought over the best way to arrange an encounter and finally turned with his request to
the Bernsteins. Max Bernstein, a royal counselor and a
very well-known lawyer in Munich, had defended Maximilian Harden in the Eulenburg case. Elsa Bernstein was
a writer and, under the name of Ernst Rosmer, had
written the libretto for Humperdinck's *The King's
Children*. It was a cultivated, intellectual salon that she
presided over. So Thomas Mann turned to her for an
introduction: "You know the Pringsheims well. Couldn't
you invite me with Katia Pringsheim some time so that
I can finally meet her?"

Frau Bernstein said, "There's nothing simpler. I'll
invite you both for dinner."

Then she told my parents she would like to invite
Katia some time (with no ulterior motives). Actually
the Bernsteins had invited Thomas Mann as well and

had cleverly seated us side by side. It was so nice of her.

Frau Bernstein, who eagerly encouraged our acquaintance and apparently was fond of making matches, enthusiastically invited us both again. From then on we got to know each other well, and things began to take shape. After the episode in the streetcar Thomas Mann had decided: this one or no one. At first I didn't take it very seriously, but it all came about anyway.

He came to visit us too. My mother realized rather soon what was going on as far as he was concerned and didn't have anything against it, for she liked him very much. She had a high opinion of him right from the start and thought it would be fine. She was also capable of properly appreciating his literary accomplishments.

Then one morning he arrived and said that I had promised we would take a bike ride together. I hadn't said anything of the sort, but it was a beautiful day, and so I said we could. We took our ride. I had a very good, fast American Cleveland bike and rushed off ahead of him. He described our ride a bit in *Royal Highness*, except that the ordinary bicycle has been transformed there into a horse: Imma Spoelmann rides off in front of Prince Klaus Heinrich.

In short, we saw each other frequently and got better acquainted and became close friends.

We had a servant who came from what were then the eastern provinces of Austria. Ignatz always called me Fräulein Katju—I don't know why. And whenever Thomas Mann came, Ignatz whispered to him, "Fräulein Katju is in the garden." So our romance was also encouraged by the servant. And the opinion of our family's friendly bookseller Buchholz was likewise very reassuring for my parents, especially for my father, who didn't concern himself much with "literature" but tended to read scholarly things. I don't even know whether he had read *Buddenbrooks;* in any case he wasn't very well acquainted with it, and he didn't have a very high opinion of Schopenhauer's philosophy, which plays a vital role in the novel. On the other hand, my father and his son-in-law were in accord in their passionate admiration for Richard Wagner.

My father took a critical stand toward Schopenhauer because the philosopher repeatedly made deprecating remarks about mathematics. As a member of the Bavarian Academy of Sciences, Father had once given a lecture entitled "Schopenhauer and Mathematics" at one of their meetings, pointing out that Schopenhauer had really understood nothing about the subject and that his pronouncements about it were wrong. My husband, however, didn't know about this, and I never told him about it either. My father had given it when I was a child.

Well, when my mother went to Herr Buchholz's store one day and asked about books by Thomas Mann —he certainly must have some on hand—he said, "Thomas Mann? Oh, yes. He will certainly make at least as much of a name for himself as Gottfried Keller. I can tell you that." That was very encouraging for my parents, wasn't it? But, as I have said, my father still was not enthusiastic, and I, although for other reasons, wasn't either and behaved quite skeptically. At first there was some resistance on my part; I had no intention of marrying so young. I said, "But we don't know each other well enough yet!"

I was twenty and was quite happy with my existence: with my studies, my brothers, the tennis club, everything. I was content and really didn't see why I should leave it all so quickly. But Thomas Mann desperately wanted to marry me. It was obvious, and he went about it quite dashingly, I might say. He wasn't at all a difficult suitor though, and the letters he wrote to me in the summer of 1904, when we were separated for several months on account of my father's illness and a trip to the Baltic, were very passionate by his standards. My mother and I accompanied my father, who was quite ill, to Kissingen; after that I went to the Baltic with my twin brother. The two of us were always deposited there when my parents went on extended bicycle tours with the three older children. Auto trips were not yet known at that time. They rode through all of Europe, pedaling from Munich to Oslo (it was still called Christiania then) or to southern Italy. In the meantime my brother Klaus and I were peacefully settled on the Baltic, and Thomas Mann wrote me wonderfully beautiful letters there—he *did* know how to write—which naturally impressed me, but which I didn't answer quite so beautifully.

When I came back—it must have been in September—it wasn't very long at all before we became engaged. The wedding took place on February 11 of the following year (1905). By that time I was twenty-one.

My twin brother, Klaus, was strongly in favor of

the marriage. All his life he boasted that he had brought it about; that is of course ridiculous, but he did support it from the first. I must confess that in the beginning my brothers always called Thomas Mann "the liverish cavalry officer" because he was rather pale and slim, and then too he was so very correct, with his mustache and in his whole bearing. But they didn't mean it maliciously. No one was really against the marriage. Urmiemchen was also in complete agreement, although she was still a little disappointed because I hadn't finished my studies and received a degree. For this is what, as an advocate of women's rights, she had hoped for me. But after all, she could only have welcomed such a grandson-in-law, couldn't she? If I had to get married at all, Thomas Mann was undoubtedly the right man in her eyes. She had a great sensitivity to literature and knew about his works. In addition, she was a terribly good and kind woman, who would never have opposed anything, unless it had been ugly.

When we were engaged, we went to Berlin and were feted as a betrothed couple by my relatives there. On this occasion Thomas Mann was scheduled to give a reading at the Verein für Kunst. This was a literary society headed by Else Lasker-Schüler's husband, who must have been something of a composer too, for at the beginning of this reading he played a piece called "Thomas Mann." It was a very strange buzzing on the cello. I have always been prone to laughter, and I got a fit of hysterics. In order to calm me down, Frau Lasker-Schüler kept throwing chocolates at me, which only made me laugh all the more. Somehow we managed to get through it—the combination of the cello and my laughter.

Thomas Mann read from *Fiorenza*. A critic wrote that it was somewhat peculiar to hear these Renaissance dialogues delivered in North German dialect; this was very unjust, however, because Thomas Mann didn't have a strong North German accent, only a very slight one. But you know how critics are. They knew that he was from Lübeck, and so they thought they had to pin that label on him. (To be sure, it was not as bad as Kerr's criticisms.) Then the lecture fee wasn't paid either, and from Munich Thomas Mann wrote the society a letter which he showed to me: "I must reluctantly call to your attention the fact that you have not yet sent me the fee of 100 marks which you owe me. I urgently request that you do so now. This is not a matter of greed on my part but of honor, because I am convinced that Wolzogen received his fee immediately."

I said, "How can you write such a thing? Their reply will be: 'Rest assured: Wolzogen didn't get his fee either.' So you must write, 'I insist upon your paying me.' But I would leave out the business about Wolzogen." As far as I can remember, he got his fee. So much for the reading in Berlin.

On this first trip of ours, we were also invited to visit my uncle Hermann Rosenberg, who was the president of the Berlin Bank Society and who had a very lovely house on a private street off Tiergartenstrasse. A dinner was given in honor of the engaged couple, and one of the guests was Maximilian Harden, with whom my mother was on very good terms. The next day he said to her, "It was truly a joy to see such attractive young people." That irritated my husband. He didn't want to be included with "attractive young people."

Then we visited my paternal grandparents, who were very wealthy. Their very first question was, "Well, Tommy, what would you like us to give you?" And he answered, "Well, I really don't have a very good watch." They said they would immediately notify the best jeweler in Berlin, whereupon a selection of splendid gold watches arrived. He was given a Glashütter gold watch, which has never had to be cleaned and which is still in the family today. Nowadays you continually have to be running to the watchmaker, but watches were different then. Now I have passed it on to my son Golo.

That was our first trip to Berlin. The second took place when I was already expecting our first child. We visited my grandmother Dohm, the advocate of women's rights, and the way my husband behaved with her wasn't very tactful at all. She asked him, "Well, Tommy, what do you want, a boy or a girl?" He said, "A boy, of course. After all, a girl is not to be taken seriously." That was bad. But in spite of it they got along very well together.

It turned out to be a girl, Erika. I was very annoyed. I have always been annoyed when it was a girl. I don't know why. Altogether we had three boys and three girls, so there was a balance. If it had been four girls and two boys, I would have been beside myself, but this way it was all right. Although he thought a girl wasn't to be taken seriously, my husband was more favorably disposed toward the girls. Erika was always his favorite; and next came Elisabeth, the youngest; Monika not to the same extent. Erika and Elisabeth were definitely his favorites among his children; they were decidedly closer to him than the sons.

Our first home was in Schwabing, Franz Joseph-strasse 2. My father furnished it handsomely for us while we were on our honeymoon in Zurich and Lucerne. It was February, and we were away a good two weeks. When we returned, our first home was waiting for us. My father had a special liking for the style of the Italian Renaissance, and he had great fun doing the decorating. But these quarters soon became too small. Erika, Klaus, Golo, and Monika arrived, and there just wasn't enough room for four children. So we rented a spacious semi-detached house in Herzogpark, at that time a very attractive section on the Isar, and here, on Mauerkircher-strasse, there was room for everybody. The two youngest children hadn't been born then.

We might have laid claim to a house in Lübeck which the Mann heirs had inherited. It was an attractive brick building with white shutters, on the outskirts of the city. Once when we were in Lübeck, we took a look at it with a distant cousin of my husband's who was a businessman, a merchant. It was my first visit to Lübeck. The city was of course still intact in those days, whereas since then much of it has been destroyed. It meant a lot to me to see it, partly on account of *Buddenbrooks* of course, but also because it was my husband's birthplace, although I didn't find the Hanseatic or North

German element in his personality at all noticeable. I said to him, "It wouldn't be such a bad idea to move here. It's charming." But the cousin said, "Oh, I think you would miss the cultural fare." Nothing came of it, and later we built a house in the Bogenhausen section of Munich, where we continued to enjoy sufficient "cultural fare." The house, at Poschingerstrasse 1, was a little bit like our present house in Kilchberg, only considerably larger. Indeed, it had to be.

Thomas Mann's relationship with Lübeck—or rather the relationship of the people of Lübeck with Thomas Mann—was, his life long, a chapter in itself. Like Frau Senator Mann, his mother, like Gerda and Hanno Buddenbrook, like Tonio Kröger, he was a rare bird there. He loved his mother very much and was enormously attached to her. When I met her, she was no longer very beautiful, but you could see that she had once been. She had fine features, was a southern type, half Brazilian—her Brazilian mother, who died young, must also have been beautiful. After that, when still a small child, she came with her father on his return to Lübeck, and went to the private school that my husband describes in *Buddenbrooks;* I guess things there really were as they are in Sesemi Weichbrodt's school, with the "sugar bowl" and all. Then, at an early age the foreign girl married Senator or Consul Heinrich Mann. She had definite artistic talents, played the piano quite nicely, and sang. My husband learned the entire literature of the German Lied from his mother. While she played and sang, he was permitted to be present, just like little Hanno. She also had a talent for drawing. If a portrait was painted of someone in the family and it didn't please her, she "improved" it. Whether that helped the portrait at all, I don't know, but I do know that she simply touched it up a little. In short, she was gifted and beautiful.

In Munich, where she and the children moved after the death of Senator Mann, she was still quite full of joie de vivre. She entertained a circle of various gentlemen—art historians, a numismatist, and others—and these gentlemen were always undecided as to whether they should court the daughters or the mother. The daughters were a little pained because their mother still placed such emphasis on her feminine charms and had admirers. A certain Dr. Löhr was also a guest there—a highly educated, pleasant little figure of a man—and he too was always undecided, I believe, between the mother and the daughter Lula, my husband's older sister, whose real name was Julia. He finally married the daughter after all. However, it was not a love match but a marriage of convenience. He had a very good position as a bank president. By the time we got married, my husband's mother was already living in Augsburg.

Apropos Augsburg: that reminds me of a story about the beautiful Anna Maria Derleth and Frau Senator Mann. But first I probably should go back a little, since the name Derleth is no longer as well known today as it once was. The beautiful Anna Maria was the sister of Ludwig Derleth, a George disciple who was not as misogynistic as the master. I myself experienced Stefan George a few times. I met him at the home of my uncle by marriage, Bondi, the publisher of George and his circle. There he seemed quite natural and down to earth, not at all pompous. But then, at a soirée at Wolfskehl's, he sat enthroned and didn't want to take any notice of my mother. He even turned his back on her. She was supposed to be introduced to him, and he turned away as if to say: "What's this lady to me?"

Now, Ludwig Derleth wasn't like that. I knew him very well, and he often visited us. He was a passionate admirer of Napoleon. There is a faint echo of that in my husband's story "At the Prophet's," which he had written after a reading by Derleth and intended as a "little tribute" to my mother, as "insurance" during his courtship and waiting period, before I went away for the summer.

Ludwig Derleth was a strange man indeed. He also called me "the princess," in very soft accents. He always treated me with the greatest respect, and said, "A mistake has been made! The princess shouldn't have got married." He did not approve. At that time he wasn't yet settled in Switzerland, but lived in a number of places, including Paris for a time.

On Sundays we always had a crowd of young people for tea, and the beautiful Anna Maria often came too. One day she arrived and said, "My brother is in Paris. He is living in the rue Bonaparte!" They both had a way of trying to turn everything into something remarkable and marvelous and intense. For instance, they didn't say red wine, but crimson wine.

Anna Maria Derleth also knew my mother-in-law, who was in Augsburg at that time. On another occasion she came to tea and said, "I've come to take my leave."

"Oh, are you going on a trip? Where are you going?"

"To Augsburg. I think I shall stay the night."

She always expressed herself that way. The whole thing, however, was simply that she wanted to pay her respects to Frau Senator Mann and tell her about us.

From Augsburg my mother-in-law moved to the country, to Polling, where people by the name of Schweighardt lived (my husband more or less glamorized them under the name of Schweigestill in *Dr. Faustus*). There she lived only for her children and her memories.

She was closer to Thomas Mann—and probably to his older brother, Heinrich—than their father was. And in turn I think my husband was closer to his father than Heinrich was. Thomas Mann esteemed his father highly and basically modeled the character of Thomas Buddenbrook after him, naturally imparting to that fictional figure many of his own characteristics as well. His father must have been a very talented man, poised and active in society. I think my husband was sorry to have disappointed him in a way, because he had been such a poor student and wasn't at all suited for the business which he was expected to enter. Upon the death of its head, the company was dissolved.

II

THE RELATIONSHIP between the two brothers was a strange one from the beginning. Once when they were still in Lübeck, Thomas and Heinrich, who were four years apart, didn't speak to each other for a whole year (I learned this from my husband himself). I don't know the reason for their silence at that time. Somehow or other they were simply incompatible. Heinrich was first supposed to become a book dealer when he finished school. Then he changed over to publishing with S. Fischer in Berlin, but one day he gave notice in order to go to Italy. My husband stayed in Lübeck to take the qualifying examination for one year's military service only; it is a well-known fact that his formal education ended at that point. His mother was already living in Munich with her three younger children, and he followed her there. In those days, as his letters reveal, he was apparently very attached to Heinrich. He wanted to join him in Florence and wrote to him, "It would really be a shame if you leave before I get there, and I hope to goodness that we manage to meet." During the year they spent together in Rome and Palestrina they were on very good terms; my husband was perhaps even influenced by Heinrich to a certain extent.

It was a relationship that fluctuated between affection and aversion, but it was the aversion that came to predominate over the years. I didn't get to know Heinrich until after we were married. We had a very odd relationship: we used the formal mode of address with each other all our lives. Heinrich was probably the strangest man you can imagine. He was very formal—a mixture of extreme reserve and, at the same time, of abandon. I could imitate his slightly affected, precise tone well, and I always loved doing so. One of my lines was, "Ah, the rich! How well off they are."

But I was actually very good friends with him, except that we were always arguing up until the time of the First World War. To annoy him, I usually took the side of the Russian generals. But the brothers were growing apart then, politically too, for Heinrich's orientation was completely toward the French-Latin tradition, whereas my husband's cultural roots were German, thoroughly German.

Thomas Mann didn't have a very strong affinity for French literature. He read French with some effort, and not very frequently. Scandinavian and, above all, Russian literature were much closer to his heart.

The break came with Heinrich's essay on Zola; it caused them both much suffering, though which one suffered more from this fraternal hostility is hard to say. This unfortunate essay began in a truly offensive way, if you recall: "It is a characteristic of those who are to dry up at an early age that they are already on the scene

in their early twenties with a high degree of conscious-
ness and worldly wisdom." No one was more aware
than my husband himself that he was the target of this
barb. It wounded him beyond all measure, and he took
this first part of the essay far more to heart than was
really necessary, since Heinrich's polemics didn't catch
him off guard. The brothers had already argued repeatedly because Heinrich was so completely oriented
toward the West. My husband, on the other hand, even
though he had not been nationalistic until the outbreak
of the First World War, did change his earlier position
as a result of that war. For a time he believed in the
legends of the ill will of other nations toward Germany,
of its encirclement, and of its downfall and destruction.
But without Heinrich's Zola essay my husband would
never have written *Reflections of a Nonpolitical Man.*
The whole thing was passionate polemics directed
against his brother, since the idea of the "Zivilisations-
literat" (a literary advocate of "civilization"), who is
more or less meant to stand for Heinrich, dominates the
book for long stretches. At the same time, in the course
of writing the book, Thomas Mann gradually freed
himself from the ideas which had held sway over him.
In the introduction, which was written last, he had already gained distance, referring to his own "rear-guard
action" and stating with conviction that what will and
must come is democracy. He wrote *Reflections* in all
sincerity and, in so doing, ended by getting over what
he had advocated in the book. The fraternal quarrel was
settled, and a reconciliation took place when Heinrich
fell seriously ill in January 1922.

. . .

During the First World War it was very difficult to feed a family with four growing children decently, and I didn't have an easy time. I literally spent the whole day riding around Munich on my bicycle to find provisions wherever I could. At first, we definitely didn't want to have anything to do with the black market, but finally we just couldn't manage anymore. Moreover, people kept making us special offers which were very tempting. Once a boy who was seventeen at most came to us and said, "If you ever need anything, I could probably get it for you." And I said, "Yes, we may need this or that in the way of food." Then every once in a while he brought us a little butter, a few eggs, and so on. I was expecting my youngest daughter at that time, and the very next year along came my youngest son. It was then that the boy looked at me very sternly and said, "So soon again, Frau Doktor? I can't feed that one too!" Of all my "suppliers," my favorite was this young boy who had reproached me about the additional baby.

The heating situation was also precarious. We had a man who called himself Hirschbethelo von Rosenstein, I don't know why; he told us he could supply us with coal, only I would have to come and discuss it with him, and he gave me his address. So I rode there on my bicycle, climbed four flights of stairs, and there lay the fellow in bed, saying, "Just sit right down on my bed, Frau Mann." I felt quite uncomfortable; finally he said he would deliver the coal. Late one evening he came and dumped it on the street and went off again. So we had to shovel it up secretly at dead of night and get it into the cellar. It was really a difficult time.

Worse things were to follow: people were forced to rent out their spare rooms. With five children in the house we were supposed to take in a lodger. The year after that the sixth baby arrived. I went to the housing office and said, "Now we don't have to take in a lodger; we have another new baby." Whereupon the official replied, "You had no right to do that!" Such experiences were typical of those days.

During the war we sold our country house in Tölz. It was the first house we had built and furnished ourselves, the California one in Pacific Palisades being the fourth and last. We usually got into financial difficulties when we were building, and they had to be solved one way or another. My husband had never in his whole life asked for an advance from a publisher: he said he found it depressing. But in the case of the country house in Tölz, he turned to his publisher Sami Fischer after some hesitation to ask for one.

He wrote him a long, detailed letter saying we had had more expenses than anticipated, that we were really quite short at the moment, but that *Royal Highness* would be appearing soon now; besides, Fischer had many connections with foreign publishers, and good receipts were certainly to be expected again. To come to the point, he would appreciate it very much if Fischer could advance him 3,000 marks.

Sami Fischer replied in the affirmative by return mail, but with one objection. "You must have made a mistake. Of course you meant 30,000 marks." For he

couldn't imagine that an author who had been so successful would write such a long, detailed letter, complete
with motivations and apologies, on account of 3,000
marks. This episode characterizes them both nicely; the
great modesty of the one and the true helpfulness and
friendly consideration of the other.

I got along well with Fischer, whom I liked very
much. I often had arguments with him, but that's only
normal when you're negotiating. I didn't want my husband to have to do the negotiating, and whenever I
appeared, Fischer's first words were always: "Well,
what dagger do you have hidden in your dress today?"
There was a great controversy over the popular edition
of *Buddenbrooks*. Droemer had had the idea of an inexpensive edition at a discount price of 2.85 marks. His
publishing house (Knaur) put out two inexpensive series, one comprising "Novels of the World" and the
other, classical works of world literature. *Buddenbrooks*
was supposed to appear in this second series as the only
book by a living author, in an edition of one million
copies, and Droemer offered to pay us 100,000 marks
for it. But Fischer refused to give permission for this
special edition; he turned it down flat. So we made a
special trip to Berlin to talk to him and try to reach
an agreement, and Tommy said to him, "Herr Fischer,
I need it. I can use the money only too well. I can't
throw an amount like that to the wind, and since you
won't do it, I'm very much in favor of Droemer's doing
it. So much for the materialistic side. As far as the
idealistic side is concerned, you must see that times have
changed. New times have to be taken into account, and

the popular edition of a book that has proved itself for a whole generation may be a new experience for a publishing house like S. Fischer, but it is by no means dishonorable. There is certainly nothing demeaning about it which would shake the book trade to its foundations—such a move is simply in keeping with the times. Moreover, an inexpensive mass printing would reach an entirely different public."

Fischer: "There is only *one* public."

"You can't say that," I protested. "There are students, shop girls, and many, many others who can't afford Fischer books. And what if they go and buy them from Droemer? That doesn't hurt you at all."

"Then I'll do it myself."

And it was a tremendous success. Fischer's press in Leipzig soon couldn't keep up with the printing and reprinting; little provincial presses without so much business had to help out. Everywhere the rotary presses were turning out nothing but *Buddenbrooks*, and many Leipzig binderies were working on it simultaneously. On publication day a motorcade of forty trucks made the deliveries to the Berlin bookstores. This book parade was featured in all the illustrated journals. It was a sensation and a gigantic success, and naturally at the same time brought a very substantial profit to the publisher as well as to us. But at first Fischer had wanted to hear nothing of it. He was that stubborn, and in such cases I had it out with him "with the dagger hidden in my dress"—but I still liked him very much.

III

WE KEPT what you might call open house in Munich, and many of our friends were more or less frequent guests there. It would be hard for me today to list them all by name—Hesse, Hofmannsthal, Hauptmann, Joseph Ponten, Bruno Frank, Ernst Bertram, Gide, Wedekind, Heinrich Mann, Bruno Walter, Gustav Mahler, Furtwängler, and many, many others. The friends we didn't see in Munich we corresponded with or met on our travels in Germany and abroad.

While we were living in Germany, my husband went on many lecture tours around the country, which often kept us apart for long periods. On the one hand, I couldn't accompany him because of the children; on the other hand, for health reasons I was often away myself for long periods; and besides, his German tours didn't interest me very much anyway. But I always went with him on his trips abroad. We were in Venice and Vienna together several times during the course of the years, also in Holland, England, Paris (about which he wrote his *Paris Report*), and many other places in Europe, and of course I was with him in Stockholm in 1929, when he received the Nobel Prize.

He liked to travel, and so did I, when I wasn't worrying about the children, my parents, and the household. We both loved Vienna, and in those days it still had a colony of writers. We knew them all: Hofmannsthal, whom we already knew from Munich; Schnitzler, who had a very winning and confidence-inspiring way about him. Perhaps that was because he was actually a doctor by profession. My husband liked him very much, and there was something in each of Schnitzler's books that was of special interest to him. *Leutnant Gustl* in particular is an excellent novella. Then there was Beer-Hofmann, whom I didn't know very well myself. Musil we didn't know personally, but my husband was one of the first to write a favorable review of *The Man Without Qualities,* and Musil thanked him for it by writing very mean things about him in later years. My husband regarded Hofmannsthal very highly. Of the contemporary writers of his and our generation, perhaps he valued him even more than Hermann Hesse, of whom he was especially fond. It's hard to judge, but I do think Hesse was his favorite. Thomas Mann had read *Demian* with great interest, of course without knowing Hesse was hiding behind the pseudonym "Sinclair"; he had inquired among his friends about this unknown Sinclair and had asked S. Fischer, who told him that Hesse had delivered the manuscript for Sinclair, an ailing young poet in Switzerland who didn't wish to be disturbed. Thomas Mann thought it was a shame. He wanted to let Sinclair know how exceptionally well he had liked *Demian.*

In the beginning of the twenties we met Hesse in

Munich, where he visited us with Ninon Dolbin, later to be his wife. We became very good friends, and my husband personally found him especially congenial. Hesse had a great deal of human understanding in his droll way, a good sense of humor—something my husband always loved—and he was a good conversationalist, who liked to sit and chat.

My husband had the feeling that *The Glass Bead Game* was a companion piece to *Dr. Faustus.* I can't quite see it that way myself. The marked relationship he thought he found there I don't see at all. In any case, he thought very highly of Hesse's works, and using the right of former winners of the Nobel Prize to submit their recommendations, he insisted that Hesse should be awarded the prize too.

Thomas Mann liked René Schickele and also liked to read him. Bruno Frank was his friend, and he prized his talent as well. Werfel he liked very much on human terms and held him in high regard, but not Stefan Zweig. He thought very highly of Gerhart Hauptmann, but more so as a dramatist than as a novelist. Hauptmann! Goodness, he was splendid. We saw him frequently. My husband had known him earlier, having seen him at S. Fischer in Berlin; I remember mainly our meetings in Bolzano, in Munich, and at Hiddensee.* We were in Bolzano together for two weeks. Hauptmann made a big impression on my husband because of his strange, somewhat inarticulate way of speaking. There was something rather vague about him. He didn't quite manage to get the things out that he wanted to say. He

* An island in the Baltic where Hauptmann is buried.

was an imposing character, and my husband became aware of it on that occasion, for while we were still in Bolzano he said to me, regarding *The Magic Mountain,* "You know, I've never been sure who it was Madame Chauchat should come back to Davos with. She has to come back with a companion, but with whom? Now I know."

Then I realized whom he meant. That fragmentary way of speaking and those convincing gestures that Mynheer Peeperkorn has in *The Magic Mountain* in reality belonged to Hauptmann. His wife, Margarete, once said to me later that Peeperkorn was surely the finest of tributes to Gerhart.

He was exceedingly obliging and kind to me. I still remember I wanted to return to Munich because the two youngest children were still very small, and they had a new nurse. "You know, Tommy," I said, "we really should go home now."

Margarete was shocked and said, "I must say, Gerhart, if you were having a good time somewhere, I would never insist on leaving."

Hauptmann: "But Margarete, think of the children, of the little ones."

He understood perfectly, and moreover he was very taken with me in Bolzano. Once we were walking home together, two by two. My husband was walking with Margarete, Hauptmann with me, and he was rather forward, but later he said to my husband, "You know, walking with your wife—it made me all flustered." I was always on a friendly footing with him.

Our association at Hiddensee was somewhat irritating because Hauptmann was the "king" of the

island. He had urged us to go there, but he was so
clearly number one that little attention was paid to us.
We stayed in "The House by the Sea," "his" house,
but we had to eat with the other guests in the dining
room, where the food was mediocre, whereas elegant
meals were brought up to Hauptmann in his rooms. The
whole thing was rather annoying.

Another time, when he was in Munich, all of us—
Hauptmann, my sister-in-law, Frau Julia Löhr, who was
very affected, and the two of us—were driving home in
our car, a rather large one. Hauptmann was acting
rather foolishly because he had been drinking as usual,
and when my sister-in-law got out, he said to her,
"Goodbye, good woman." She was deeply insulted.
She said to her brother, "I thought that one said 'good
woman' only to the cleaning woman, didn't you?" She
laid great emphasis on good manners, à la Lübeck. My
husband used her to a certain extent in *Dr. Faustus* in
the figure of one of the two Rodde sisters.

When Hauptmann turned seventy, he celebrated
for a whole year, from one city to the next, and one day
Munich had its turn too. First we had luncheon in a
small group: Max Halbe, his wife, and the two of us
were present; the champagne was flowing, and Hauptmann was in high spirits. It was then that he came within
a hair of a "brotherhood drink" with my husband, for
he started to say, "Well, Herr Mann—I mean—we two,
we are after all—we are brothers after all, so we
could . . . couldn't we? In short: enough."

He didn't finish what he was going to say, but he
was marvelous. They never did say "du" to each other.

He was always making such speeches: "Well, I mean, war? War? Horrible! But I must say: war!"

And so it went till 6 P.M.; then we went home to change our clothes. In Hauptmann's honor a special performance of his play *The Rats* had been scheduled for that evening, and Richard Billinger, a writer of peasant background, who had written a play called *Raw Night*, was going to give an introduction first. (Billinger was later imprisoned by the Nazis, and anyone who wanted to send him anything had to write down "unnatural acts" as the reason for his arrest.) Billinger couldn't begin his speech, the curtain couldn't go up, everyone was waiting, for Hauptmann was missing. The performance was supposed to begin at eight o'clock, but the guest of honor didn't come and didn't come. He was sleeping it off. Finally he appeared a half hour late, and there was a very good performance of *The Rats* after all. We sat in a box with him, and again he was very forward but very nice. He had a weakness for me. There was never an opportunity to see him after that. The times and our differing views came between. We emigrated—it was impossible for my husband not to detach himself from Nazi Germany; Hauptmann remained.

Chance found the two of them together again in Zurich, but there was no desire on either side for a meeting. In a store, the London House, on the Bahnhofstrasse, my husband was upstairs trying on a suit when the salesman came and asked, "Do you know who is downstairs? Herr Gerhart Hauptmann. Would you like to see him?" My husband said, "Oh, I think perhaps we had better wait for other times." Then the salesman replied, "That's exactly what Hauptmann said too."

In spite of everything, his death affected my husband deeply. His wife once described the circumstances to us in Gastein: how the Russians were occupying Agnetendorf, how they spared their house and allowed them to leave. He died under very sad conditions, but sad as they were, everything might well have been much worse.

Bruno Walter was one of our best friends. In 1913 he came from Vienna to be Felix Mottl's successor in Munich. He spent many long years there as Royal Bavarian general music director and artistic director of the Munich Court Opera until the rising wave of National Socialism and anti-Semitism forced him to resign his position at an early date and begin his wanderings. We were neighbors in Herzogpark. Several families who were friendly with one another lived in this section. We met Bruno Walter in the funniest way. His children, two girls, went to elementary school, Ebermayer's private school, with Erika and Klaus. Because it was quite far from Herzogpark, it had been arranged that the governesses should take turns accompanying the children to school and bringing them home again. The Walters had just moved in; we didn't know Bruno Walter personally yet when he called up one day. I said, "I'm glad to know you, Herr Walter. What can I do for you?"

"Well, I just wanted to say that it's simply unheard

of for your Klaus to pull my Gretel's hair on the way to school. That's what he did today, and it really shouldn't happen, should it? I was very much surprised that Klaus is allowed to do things like that."

I replied, "This is news to me, and you can be sure that I'll do something about it. We'll speak to Klaus, and he certainly won't do it again. I'm sorry, Herr Walter, it won't happen again."

That was our first encounter—we were close friends for the rest of our lives. He was a very concerned father. His daughter Gretel was an especially charming child; so was Klaus, I might add. It was only when he went to Dr. Ceconi, the dentist, that he was unmanageable. "You're a regular brat," the dentist used to say to him.

Bruno Walter directed the Akademie Concerts given by the Court Orchestra, which was the same as the Opera Orchestra. He was always driven to the concerts in a court carriage drawn by two horses—there was a coachman in blue livery, with a servant beside him. Since we lived nearby and also went to the concerts, he usually picked us up, and thus we had the privilege of going to the Akademie Concerts in the court carriage and pair.

Walter was a stimulating, high-spirited, nice man. There was something disarming about him, and in a certain sense he was also naïve. Naturally he was intelligent, too, but he tended to get carried away. He was born with music in him. It always surprised me—and I asked myself continually how it was possible—that music could thrill a person so completely and always engulf him anew. Whenever he rehearsed a work, an opera, a symphony, a concerto, he was totally caught up in it. He threw himself into the piece, and then it became something magnificent for him. He prized it, loved it, admired it, enthused over it. And when he visited us, he played the piano for hours, singing, explaining the action, or pointing out especially beautiful parts: "This passage—before I go—I must call it to your attention." Then came the excerpt, and he sang along with it.

He did that often. He was such a stimulating man. Also, as a young man, he had a great sensitivity for the new music. In his memoirs, *Theme and Variations*, he tells how he offended the people at the conservatory in Berlin because he spoke out strongly for Wagner, which was not yet permissible in those days. Later he spoke out vehemently for Gustav Mahler, whom he admired immensely. Rightly so.

Perhaps my husband was still playing at that time. He played the violin, had quite a good instrument, and didn't play so badly either. But his technique wasn't good, and as time went by he became less and less satisfied with it. He hated being a dilettante, but he didn't have time to practice. So he gave it up. But sometimes he would still play Beethoven sonatas with Ernst Bertram, who was a family friend during those years and the godfather of Elisabeth, our next-to-youngest child. Later the violin was given to our son Michael.

My husband couldn't really play the piano well, but he played by ear a little, improvised, and when he played, he inevitably played *Tristan*. He loved music, and if you want to divide people into eye and ear types, he really wasn't an eye type, except of course that he was always able to get a complete picture of a person at a glance.

His greatest interest in the arts, outside of literature, was undoubtedly always in music; this naturally affected the theme and structure of all his works. He didn't have a very lively interest in painting. To be sure, he knew a good picture when he saw one, and he liked to go to galleries, but painting took third place with him. Number two was sculpture; number one, music. He always said that if he were ever born again, he would like to be a conductor. I don't know if that will ever happen, but you never can tell. Once when he said this to Bruno Walter, the conductor replied, "Oh, it's really all right the way it is too." And in Walter's book he had this to say about the writer: "Thomas Mann and music! Doesn't it dominate him more than he himself realizes?"

Interjections from Outside

G.M.: We were very friendly with Bruno Walter's children, especially my older brother and sister. It was mainly a "teenage" friendship, I would say, and therefore extremely intense. They put on plays together too.
K.M.: But that was somewhat earlier, and you used to play parts too. They—the Walters, the Hallgartens, and my children—had a theater club they called the "Mimik-Bund," and they put on performances which one of the adults usually had to write a review of. They did *As You Like It*, *Minna von Barnhelm*, and various

other things. Golo played the Lady in Mourning in
Minna. I'll never forget it: "Accept my tears and the
reward of Heaven." You were incomparable as the Lady
in Mourning, eight years old and lisping. My husband
wrote a review of it which hasn't been published. We
still have the "Mimik-Book." It didn't get lost like the
other one, the "Picture Book," which Heinrich and
Thomas did for the confirmation of their sister Carla
and which was immensely funny. Their younger brother
Vico took it, and it got lost somewhere.

G.M.: Bruno Walter also tells about the Lady in Mourning in *Theme and Variations.* The review of our first
play, *The Governess* by Theodor Körner, has even been
printed in the new complete edition of Thomas Mann's
works. It's a charming thing, done in the manner of a
Goethe parody, which we naturally didn't realize at the
time—awfully nice, paternal, and full of irony and delightful formulations.

K.M.: He could be very funny indeed. Did you have a
part in that one too?

G.M.: No. It has only three roles. Played by Erika,
Klaus, and our neighbor Ricki Hallgarten.

I shouldn't really raise the question in my mother's
presence whether our upbringing was very strict or not.
Those were other times; after all, my parents grew up
in the last century.

K.M.: Well, I wasn't all that strict. I was often a bit impatient. I used to help the children with their lessons. If
they didn't understand something right away, I got a bit
annoyed.

G.M.: Anyway, my father's work schedule was the main

thing in the house. Perhaps we all suffered a little from that.

K.M.: All in all, they had a very nice childhood. The very fact that there were so many of them and that they got along so well together meant that there was always companionship for everyone. Our house was large, and they could be pretty much on their own in the rooms on the fourth floor. In Tölz, where our country house was, there was a large yard, and then they would drive down the main street of the village in a wagon and play their games. When we took a walk in Herzogpark—the two older ones were naturally much bigger and had longer legs—Golo always said, "Klaus, don't run so fast or poor Gololo will fall down!"

G.M.: The four of us—the four older children—for a time made up a group in our area that aroused some fears. My father was very amused once when a group of children rushed toward him in wild flight, crying, "The Manns are coming! The Manns are coming!"

K.M.: You really did stick together.

G.M.: Erika and Klaus were a pair; Klaus and I were also a pair, at least for the first ten or twelve years. Then came a time when the difference in ages had too much of an effect, when I was fourteen and he was sixteen or seventeen. But in our actual childhood we played together a lot, and he always went places with me and told me about novels which he was making up and which I still remember today. He read his things to me too: in his exercise books for school he wrote dramas and comedies that he sent to the Volkstheater in Munich. He used the nom de plume "Karl Trebitsch." I don't know why he picked that one. Then I—nine years old, barefoot—had to go to the Volkstheater and say, "I'm the nephew of Karl Trebitsch, and I'm supposed to ask what you think of his play." And I actually got to see some reader or other who said, "Now where did I put that trash?" And then he gave it to me, or rather threw it at me, saying, "All right, your uncle doesn't have to stop by. Here it is." I told Klaus this, and he said, "Well, after all, he knew where the manuscript was and didn't have *that* low an opinion of me." We got along very well in those years.

K.M.: I always wanted one of my children to take up a good bourgeois profession, become a doctor or engineer, and not one of them did. Writers! A historian is all right.

G.M.: Just barely. I certainly couldn't have been an engineer; I don't know about a doctor. It's a shame—I really regret it myself that these intellectual professions continue in a family for generations. One of my nephews has become a gardener, and this pleases me very much. In any case, I always wanted to be a teacher; I was just about to get my credentials in 1933 when I was more or less forced to take a trip.

K.M.: Erika had her cabaret, "The Pepper Mill," and was an actress. Klaus was a writer; he was certainly born for that, but it wasn't a very fortunate choice for him as his father's son. It made it very hard for him; in the beginning, it made it easy, but then it made it hard. Michael was a musician and not until quite late did he become "serious," a professor of German in Berkeley.

G.M.: Now he's more serious than I am.

But you can have discipline in any job, even in the most unorthodox one, and in this respect my father very definitely set an example, and he knew it too. He always said that he didn't believe in explicit education, but that he did believe in education by example, and that, you have to grant him, was what he gave.

K.M.: I have always said too: the most important thing is the atmosphere of a home. That influences the children. And since we—my husband and I—never quarreled, and since the atmosphere was very harmonious, it was not unfavorable for the children.

G.M.: It's hard to decide whether inherited talent is more important or whether it is outweighed by growing up in a given atmosphere. The line between so-called heredity and the influences you are subjected to in life itself can't be drawn at all. The wish my mother referred to, that we, or one of us, or two of us, take up normal, practical professions, was more of a theoretical nature: that is, it wasn't expected in the atmosphere of the home or by the guests or the friends of the family. After all, they were predominantly writers, or a few of them were professors in the less remunerative fields, and people like that. We children were very strongly influenced by the table talk and other conversations we heard, and by what we read. I would say it would have involved a bold and powerful leap, perhaps even a certain amount of protest against this atmosphere, to free ourselves of it. I can remember the son of one of our good friends, the writer René Schickele, who became an oenologist or specialist in winemaking almost as a protest, I would say, against his father. But that didn't occur in our family, did it?

IV

THE CHILDREN were very independent and had their own circle, but I knew a good deal about it. The Walter and Hallgarten children along with W. E. Süskind were their Munich friends; they also went to the Wedekinds' house frequently, whereas we ourselves actually saw very little of the Wedekinds. Heinrich Mann was a close friend of Frank Wedekind. Naturally we knew Wedekind, but a close friendship between him and my husband never developed. Once they met in the Torggelstube, a Munich wine pub frequented by many writers in those days, where Wedekind had a regular table. Wedekind had apparently prepared himself for the encounter, for he said, "I have just read *Fiorenza* again. Donnerwetter! Donnerwetter!" The children were much closer, and Klaus was once even engaged to Pamela Wedekind.

It was the children who invented "the Magician." It was a long time ago, but Erika and Klaus were already grown, perhaps nineteen and twenty. I wasn't well at the time, I often had bronchitis, and the children wanted to go to a soirée at Christa Hatvany's. She was Hatvany's second wife, came from a Prussian officer's family by the name of von Winsloe, and she had written a play, a film, *Mädchen in Uniform*. She was a sculptress and had gone Bohemian. So she was giving this party, and the children said to my husband, "Why don't you come with us?" He answered, "I can't, and besides it's a costume party. What would I wear?"

They replied, "Oh, but you have that black thing for university functions, a gown, and then you can wear a fez and go as a magician. You're a magician!"

And from that time on they always called him "the Magician." It has nothing to do with the "magic feats" performed in his study or with *The Magic Mountain*.

My husband's circle of really close friends was a small one. Bruno Walter was one of them, as was Bruno Frank. The children always teased me about my Brunos. "You and your flock of Brunos," they said.

We were friendly with Emil Preetorius, and then of course with Ernst Bertram, the Germanist from Bonn, who was living in Munich at the time and had one foot in the George circle. He admired my husband very much. My husband, who disliked everything that smacked of a prophetic pose, didn't think too highly of Stefan George. But Bertram was one of my husband's oldest and best friends. It was a friendship extending back through the First World War. As far as I remember, Bertram had given a very nice lecture on *Royal Highness*. My husband, pleased at this, responded with a letter of thanks. Soon after, they met in person, and Bertram became a friend of the family. He was also very kind to the children; he was the godfather of Elisabeth, who was born during the last year of the war. *Reflections of a Nonpolitical Man*, which was written during these years, appealed to Bertram very much. Bertram was writing his Nietzsche book at the time, which my husband in turn was very fond of, and I believe this judgment didn't alter with the years.

The two men took an interest in each other's work; occasionally each read a chapter or so out loud to the other, and thus there was mutual inspiration. After the war Bertram moved more and more to the right, toward a popular nationalism, whereas my husband moved to the left, toward democracy. This gradually broke up their friendship. To be sure, my husband said at first, "His Germanistic mutterings are at the bottom of it, that's all," until this well-meaning interpretation was no longer tenable, and they grew apart altogether.

On the occasion of Gerhart Hauptmann's sixtieth birthday, in 1922, my husband gave a speech entitled "On the German Republic," which displeased Bertram greatly. It was the beginning of their alienation, but a break was avoided. After the Nazis had come to power and we were already in Switzerland, Bertram once telephoned Golo and said, "Thomas Mann absolutely must return. He belongs to Germany."

Golo replied, "Of course he does basically. But how can he? After all, my father has been attacking the Nazis for years. Under present conditions, he wouldn't be able to open his mouth."

"Why? What do you mean? After all, we're living in a free country," said Bertram.

Nazi Germany!—that was going too far. The break became complete; they didn't even correspond anymore. We didn't see Bertram again until 1954.

Another friend of the family was Joseph Ponten. His first book, *The Tower of Babylon*, a novel, was very promising, my husband thought. He wrote a nice letter to Ponten about it, and they became acquainted. Ponten was such a funny man; he was devoured by ambition, and it was the bane of his existence that he always measured himself by Thomas Mann and wanted to surpass him. But he didn't succeed.

He once said to my husband, "I am writing something now that will be 'a magic mountain.' No, it will be a whole chain of magic mountains." His plans were grandiose. He had a certain talent, but his ambition destroyed him. His projects were simply overblown. He wanted to write the history of a German family that emigrates to different parts of the world, following up its individual branches. *People on the Move: A Novel of German Unrest*, the mammoth work was supposed to be called. But it was never completed.

It was downright pathological, the way he always compared himself with Thomas Mann. Once he said to him, "I am a poet, and you are a writer. No, I am both."

He just loved to say unpleasant things to people. One occasion was the celebration of my husband's fiftieth birthday; it is the custom at such events for someone to address a few words to the wife of the guest of honor. Ponten had undertaken this task, and he did it quite nicely, I thought. Then, after dinner he asked me, "Do you know why I was chosen to give the speech?"

"No. I imagine it's because you have a very high opinion of me."

"No, they just couldn't find anybody else who would do it in all of Munich."

Ponten was in America when my husband received the Nobel Prize. He visited us on his return. My husband said something like, "Oh, well, someone has to get it. It's not such a distinction—it could happen to anyone."

Ponten: "You know, Mann, you mustn't underestimate it. When I was in America and you received the Nobel Prize, I was often asked: 'Who is Thomas Mann?'" He took a fiendish delight in saying that.

Now, the Nobel Prize did not come as a complete surprise to anyone. There had been talk about it for some time, and the previous year Thomas Mann had been named as a candidate. A Germanist, Professor Frederik Böök, had a decisive voice in the awarding of the prize. This Professor Böök didn't like *The Magic Mountain*. When the book appeared in 1924, he wrote that it was so unequivocally and exclusively German that it couldn't be translated into any foreign language —which was too bad. He wrote that to my husband too. Well, the book that "couldn't be translated into any foreign language" was translated everywhere and was clearly a universal success—my husband's first. In America today it is still "a classic." Before that, Thomas Mann was well known, it is true, but not until *The Magic Mountain* did he really attain the international reputation that gained him the prize. But the self-righteous Herr Böök was not willing to acknowledge it, and in the citation it says that Thomas Mann was awarded the prize primarily for *Buddenbrooks*. It was foolishness on Böök's part and sheer nonsense besides, since *Buddenbrooks* appeared in 1901—they could have given him the prize twenty-five years earlier. (Böök, incidentally, was quite sympathetic to the Nazis later and thus had an unpleasant time of it in Scandinavia.)

The Swedish publisher Bonnier telephoned immediately from Stockholm, and I went along for the award ceremony, for after all it was something that happens only once in a lifetime and was really very interesting. The other prize winners were there too. In physics there was a Duc de Broglie, a leading physicist from Paris. Among the recipients was an American who stood around with his hands in his pockets, saying gauchely, "I can't see any particular reason why I should have the prize, but anyway, it is a great pleasure for me to be here." Actually the feelings expressed by this future compatriot were close to those my husband later voiced to Ponten upon his return from the United States.

The actual ceremony was naturally very festive, but also very funny. There sat the king on his throne. The prize winners were all in evening dress and spoke a few words; then, one after another, when their names were called, they had to approach the throne, and King Gustav presented them with the citation. When the French duke received his citation, however, the king rose and took a few steps toward him. That struck me as wrong.

Then came the dinner, a splendid banquet. It was the custom that the king could sit only next to persons of noble blood, not next to the wife of an award winner, for example, or any of the other guests of honor. It had to be the nobility, since it was a great banquet, so there he sat between two old crones—two princesses. The table was set magnificently, a stunning damask table-cloth covered it, and we all ate from silver plates. But the king had an extra lace cloth over the damask, and he alone dined with gold utensils. There were many serv-ants passing food, but behind the king stood his own butler who served him personally. That was the custom: everyone else was waited on by different servants, but the king had to be served by his personal butler and sit in front of his golden plate between his old crones. It was funny, but it was all a great celebration, and natu-rally we were in high spirits.

A very good journalist was there, a Jewish jour-nalist from the *Berliner Tageblatt,* I think. He said to us, "You are leaving the money in Stockholm, aren't you? I hope you aren't going to take it back to Germany."

We said, "Why not? Don't we have to? We're not permitted to leave it here, are we?"

He was trying to give us some good advice. "Leave it abroad. I would definitely do so, if I were you."

Of course we lost it all, along with everything else, when we emigrated in 1933.

The year after the Nobel Prize we traveled to Egypt. My husband was already at work on *Joseph and His Brothers* and wanted to do some checking up, as it were. He had been in Egypt once before, but I think

only in Cairo. At that time the Stinnes Lines had invited
him on a Mediterranean cruise as their guest. Now, we
journeyed up the Nile as far as Aswan, and he inspected
everything that he had wanted to, and it was all as he
had imagined. We also went to Palestine, but I had already picked up amoebic dysentery in Cairo and had to
go to the hospital. My husband traveled on alone because
he had to give an address in Jerusalem. When I joined
him, he was sick, but not seriously. I had an immediate
relapse, however, and didn't see anything at all of Jerusalem. I spent the whole time in bed in the German hospital there.

V

WHEN HE WAS WRITING A BOOK, Thomas Mann never considered what effect it would have on the people he had more or less used as models. He always said to me, and rightly, "I didn't mean him at all. I simply used the traits that were right for my character."

First of all, the people of Lübeck were quite angry with him on account of *Buddenbrooks*: "a bird who soils his own nest," and so on. Then Holitscher started that ridiculous story about the field glasses; it is pure fabrication. It is true that Thomas Mann had Holitscher's physical appearance in mind when he described Detlev Spinell in "Tristan," but he never stood on the balcony looking after him with opera glasses. He didn't need to do that at all.

He shared his plans with me from the very beginning, insofar as he knew them. When we were engaged, he talked a good deal about *Fiorenza*, which he was working on at the time, and he told me about *Royal Highness* too. However, the idea for that novel did not come about as the result of his engagement and marriage. He always saw the writer's activity as somewhat representative and symbolic, and in letters to Walter Opitz and to Heinrich, he frequently mentions that there is definitely something princely about the writer's calling. To be sure, the prince's story is also the novel of the early days of our marriage. He said this later himself. And it is true, too, not in every detail but in a more general sense.

My father was an avid collector of Renaissance objets d'art, both silver and faïence. Thomas Mann changed this into a glass collection in *Royal Highness*, and he also used the rather ungracious character of my father, who was always somewhat ailing, gruff, and impatient. I would say that old Spoelmann is a more faithful portrait of my father than Imma is of me. Even though Thomas Mann primarily had me in mind, in my opinion it's a distorted portrait. Imma is a little too impertinent—I wasn't really like that. It's true that I liked to show my superiority a bit from time to time; still, Imma goes too far in my opinion—but I don't know myself that well. In short, he gave a very stylized portrait of father and daughter.

Klaus Heinrich's first encounter with Imma represents the actual incident in the streetcar when I gave the conductor a piece of my mind. The visits at teatime, the episode with the guttapercha paper, and the first horseback ride together—all are based on real events. But he left out the matchmaker, our eastern Ignatz with his "Fräulein Katju is in the garden."

Everything has been transposed, and there is a great difference in particular between Prince Klaus Heinrich and Thomas Mann. There the connections with outer reality cease, although Klaus Heinrich's relationship to Albrecht bears a certain resemblance to Thomas Mann's relationship to his brother Heinrich; also, the relationship to his older sister Lula is faintly echoed. The court officials are completely fictional.

No one held *Royal Highness* against him, but on the other hand, all the fuss about his story "Blood of the Walsungs" is much ado about nothing: my twin brother and I grew up together and were very close to each other, which is quite understandable. Klaus had a life-long attachment to my husband, who, admittedly, often used to say to him, "Klaus, you know, you're exactly what I think of as a buffoon." Klaus did have his peculiarities, but this never disturbed the relationship between the two of them.

Now, my husband had written this story about twins. First of all, the milieu was totally altered: my father was not a little parvenu like the father in the novella, but in reality a highly respected scholar and art connoisseur. The social role which my parents played in Munich bore no similarity to that of the Aarenholds in the novella. Second, the autobiographical interpretation seems to me to be absolutely ridiculous on psychological grounds alone. If Thomas Mann had had the impression that there was an illicit relationship between me and my brother, he would have broken off with me at once or would have kept it to himself, but certainly would not have told the world about it in a novella. It was as clear as day that no such thing could have been going on. But you know how people are. The gossip was terrible, and it got to my parents. My father was beside himself, and he said, "The story simply can't appear. It's scandalous!" The issue of the *Neue Rund-schau* in which the novella had been printed was withdrawn from circulation. Not until sixteen years later, in 1921, was the story given its legitimate place among the other novellas.

Thomas Mann's plans were always much more modest than their execution. *The Magic Mountain* was supposed to be a novella, *Joseph* was supposed to be a novella, and what happened? Brecht, that sly and ironic mind, wasn't so far from the truth on this point with his bon mot about "Thomas Mann, the short story writer."

His things had a will and a life of their own, and my husband never knew how extensive they would become. For example, he hadn't intended to write *Death in Venice* at all, and then, later, he didn't plan to be at work on this novella for a whole year. In the beginning he wanted to do something entirely different: what he had in mind was a novella about Goethe. He wanted to write about Goethe's last love in Marienbad. It was supposed to take the Master down a peg or two in a humorous way. But at that time he simply didn't have the nerve to portray Goethe. He didn't think he was up to such a task yet, and he transposed the Goethe novella into *Death in Venice*. *The Beloved Returns* was written much later; only then did he dare to do it.

Death in Venice is an especially interesting case insofar as all the details of the story, beginning with the man at the cemetery, are taken from actual experience. You see, in the spring of 1911 we planned to take a

Dalmatian journey. Since it had been highly recommended to us, we first went to Brioni. That's also mentioned in the story. We didn't like it much there. In the first place, it didn't have a sandy beach; and in the second place, the mother of Archduke Karl of Austria was one of the guests. This archduchess had the tasteful habit of coming in to dinner two minutes after everyone else had sat down. The guests ate in the large dining room of the hotel, table d'hôte style. Upon her entrance everyone, including foreigners, arose; then she always departed two minutes before the meal was over, whereupon everyone had to do the same all over again. It was really very bothersome and annoying.

We then took the steamer to Venice. My husband was tremendously attached to the Lido and to Venice. We often went there, but we had always come by train before. On this trip we arrived by sea for the first time, and on the ship we really did see the graying dandy, an aging man who was all spruced up and obviously wearing makeup, surrounded by young people. They were making a lot of noise and showing off.

When we arrived, we looked for a gondola to take us over to the Lido. One appeared immediately, and the gondolier said he was willing to take us. And when we got out and paid him, a bystander came up and said, "That one doesn't have a license. You're lucky that you didn't have any trouble with him." So the graying dandy was there, and so was the gondolier.

Then we went to the hotel where we had reservations—Hotel des Bains—right on the beach. It was very crowded, and in the dining room, on the very first day, we saw the Polish family, which looked exactly the way my husband described them: the girls were dressed rather stiffly and severely, and the very charming, beautiful boy of about thirteen was wearing a sailor suit with an open collar and very pretty lacings. He caught my husband's attention immediately. This boy was tremendously attractive, and my husband was always watching him with his companions on the beach. He didn't pursue him through all of Venice—that he didn't do—but the boy did fascinate him, and he thought of him often.

Heinrich, who was also in our party, kept wanting us to leave Venice for somewhere in the mountains. We were reluctant to do so, but because he was so eager to go to some place in the Apennines, we agreed. It was quite unpleasant: we stayed in a hotel without modern conveniences, which disturbed me, and in order to keep us there, the hotel owner kept saying, "That beautiful villa will be free in two days." Then we would be able to move in and everything would be wonderful.

Some English people were staying in it. Once I went up to them and asked them how things stood and when they were intending to leave.

"Oh, nothing's settled. We don't know yet."

And I said, "I would be glad to know because we are waiting for these rooms, you know."

"Oh, he's obviously playing you along."

Well, we left in a hurry and returned triumphantly to Venice. Besides, Heinrich's trunk had been lost, which was another reason for our return, and my husband was delighted to be back at the Lido. The Polish family was still staying at the hotel. One evening that somewhat obscene Neopolitan singer also appeared. Then many of the guests began to leave, and rumors were going around that there was cholera in the city. It wasn't a serious epidemic, but there were several cases. At first we didn't even know about it and didn't pay much attention to all the departures. Then we went to Cook's to arrange for our return, and the honest English clerk in the travel bureau said to us, "If I were you, I wouldn't make the sleeping-car reservations for a week from now, but for tomorrow, because, you know, several cases of cholera have broken out; naturally it's being kept secret and hushed up. We don't know how far it will spread. You must have noticed, though, that many guests in the hotel have already left." That was indeed the case, so we left too. The Polish family had already departed a day earlier.

Thus, everything was based on reality, even down to the details, but no one besides Thomas Mann would have been able to make them into *Death in Venice.* My husband transferred to Aschenbach the pleasure he actually took in this charming boy, stylizing it into extreme passion. I still remember that my uncle, Privy Counselor Friedberg, a famous professor of canon law in Leipzig, was outraged: "What a story! And a married man with a family!"

The whole thing had an interesting epilogue. *Death in Venice* was a great success, especially in America, and the novella is certainly one of my husband's best. A few years ago Erika received a letter from an elderly Polish aristocrat, a count, who wrote that something funny had happened. Some time ago friends had brought him the Polish translation of a novella in which he and his whole family were described to a T; he found this very amusing and intriguing. But he was not offended. Such was the end of the "real" story.

Outwardly, Gustave von Aschenbach bears a resemblance to Gustav Mahler. That is because my husband conceived the story in Venice when Mahler was on his deathbed. Virtually every few hours the newspapers published bulletins about his condition; every little improvement, every setback, was reported in detail, as though he were a ruling prince. Such was the honor paid to him. The way his death was mourned impressed my husband so much that he actually painted more or less of a portrait of Mahler in the physical description of Aschenbach. That was in May 1911. Later the brother of the famous physicist Max Born, Wolfgang Born, who was an artist and professor of art and art history (he later emigrated to America too), did some illustrations for *Death in Venice*, and, without knowing who the "model" was, he also gave Aschenbach the physical characteristics of Gustav Mahler. This was for an illustrated edition which was privately printed.

My parents knew Mahler, and so did we. My twin brother, Klaus, who was a musician and worshiped Mahler, joined him for a year or two at the Vienna Opera as a volunteer assistant and coach. I recall that when Mahler was in Munich for a concert, he came to our house on Mauerkircherstrasse for tea. He was so formal it was funny. I said to him, "My parents asked me to give you

(64)

their cordial greetings." To which he replied, "Please respond to them in a similar manner." I'll never forget that.

Another time we were at a rehearsal of his Eighth Symphony, whose premiere he was conducting himself in Munich. He needed some special instrument which was not regularly available in the orchestra—perhaps a glockenspiel—so it had to be borrowed from the opera. Mahler sent a messenger, and when he returned asked, "Well, where is the glockenspiel?"

"Herr Generalmusikdirektor Mottl is very sorry, but he needs it tonight himself."

To which Mahler responded, "Give Herr Generalmusikdirektor my greetings and tell him I'll perform my symphony one way or another."

My husband told me that Gustav Mahler was the first person he'd ever met who gave him the impression of being a great man. Mahler was very intense. You had the impression of an immensely strong personality; it's hard to define just where this strength lay. The elements of discipline and concentration were less evident in his case than in Aschenbach's. Those were more projections of Aschenbach's author—just as he also attributed to Aschenbach those works which he had planned to write himself but never completed.

The "Frederick" novel mentioned in the novella was a book about Frederick the Great which he never wrote. During the war he only wrote the essay "Frederick and the Great Coalition"; there were various reasons why he lost the desire to write the novel.

The "Maia" novel was only a vague plan. Two

other works, "Frederick" and "The Abject," were closer to him. He would have liked to write "The Abject." His polemic against Theodor Lessing (the philosopher and mathematician who also wrote reviews) is well known. For various reasons, he didn't think much of him. A figure à la Lessing was supposed to be the central character in "The Abject." In order to clarify the connections, I must go back a bit, back to the time of *Buddenbrooks*. When the book appeared, it wasn't a success in its first year. The critic Samuel Lublinski was the only one who was impressed by it; it was he, in his review in the *Berliner Tageblatt*, who wrote the much-quoted sentence, "This book will grow with the years and will still be read by generations to come"—which was prophetic on his part. No one else had noticed *Buddenbrooks*. As a result, my husband was extraordinarily grateful to Lublinski. He was grateful by nature, and if someone did him a good turn, he never forgot it.

Then Lublinski was insulted by Theodor Lessing in a shamelessly derogatory article. I don't remember why. It began like this: "I suppose Herr Lublinski's cradle was located in Krotoszyn," and continued in a spitefully anti-Semitic tone, which was surprising, since Lessing was Jewish himself. My husband was so furious about it that he wrote a very insulting article, "Doktor Lessing." In it he said, "Herr Lessing—we don't even know if he had a cradle—considered it appropriate to attack Herr Lublinski in this fashion. . . ." And it concluded, "What right does this disadvantaged dwarf have to be aggressive?"

Lessing was completely beside himself and sent my

husband a telegram: "I must now ask you, in the name of my family also, whether you are ready to defend yourself with weapons." My husband showed it to my father and asked, "How in the world shall I answer this fellow?"

My father said, "I would send a telegram: 'Your telegram defies all convention and is incomprehensible to me.' One sends a second, but one doesn't send a telegram to find out whether someone else is ready to fight a duel; and if, upon receiving such a preliminary inquiry, one's opponent isn't ready, does one then challenge him?"

From that time on Theodor Lessing was a deadly enemy. There was yet another reason why my husband found him so despicable. Lessing had a very pretty, tall, blond, Germanic wife, of the nobility, whom he had seduced and then married when he was a private tutor in her house. She admired his intellectual qualities. He went on to be a teacher in Haubinda, one of the first "Free Schools," where one of the students had a love affair with his wife. Lessing knew about it and tolerated it; probably not only that—he seemed to take a perverse pleasure in it as well. That's why he was "The Abject." But he did have one good idea, which would be quite timely today. He always wanted to found an anti-noise organization. That was really a very fruitful idea, because what we are subjected to today is simply incredible. We have authorities galore, but what purpose do they serve?

VI

In 1912 I had some trouble with my lungs. It was an infection, an old tubercular spot that seemed to be arrested, but I had to go to the mountains several times for my health. I was first sent to the Waldsanatorium in Davos for six months, from March to September 1912; the following year to Merano and Arosa for several months, and finally (but that was after the war) to Clavadel near Davos for another six weeks. But I was not seriously ill. My life was not in danger, and who knows, possibly the whole thing would have cleared up by itself if we hadn't been able to afford a sanatorium. It was the custom, if you had the means, to go to Davos or Arosa.

In the summer of 1912 my husband visited me in Davos and was so impressed by the whole milieu, as well as by everything I told him about it, that he immediately thought of writing a novella about the place, a sort of grotesque epilogue and a contrast to *Death in Venice*. This projected novella then turned into *The Magic Mountain*: once again a work had asserted its will.

He had also always planned a triptych: a novella about Erasmus, one about Joseph, and one about Philip II; together they were to make up a modest volume.

Here, too, the works had plans of their own. The one novella became a tetralogy, and my husband never got to the other two.

Well, he visited me in Davos, and his arrival was indeed similar to Hans Castorp's. He too got off the train in Davos-Dorf, and I met him down there, just as Castorp's cousin Ziemssen did. We went up to the sanatorium, and there we talked incessantly, like the cousins. I had already been there for months and, seizing this opportunity to let off steam, told a hundred stories and kept repeating, "It's so nice finally to have someone to talk to again."

I pointed out to him the various types whom I had already described, and he then incorporated them in the novel, merely changing their names. Two of my acquaintances, Frau Plür and her friend Frau Maus, appeared in the novel as Frau Stöhr and Frau Iltis. They really were the way Thomas Mann describes them. Priceless. Frau Plür was terribly crude, and I too was astonished (just like Hans Castorp) that someone could be so sick and at the same time so vulgar. I actually found the real names of the two ladies, Plür and Maus, much better than Stöhr and Iltis, but after all, Thomas Mann couldn't call them that.

Then I pointed out to him the "gentleman rider," the one with the ghastly cough; the melancholy Spanish woman "Tous les dé," whose eldest son was seriously ill. The second son came for a visit and immediately fell ill too. Jessen (or "Hofrat Behrens") explained it to me: "You know, the climate here is a very good remedy against illness, but under certain conditions it can also encourage it. In many cases it clearly triggers the actual outbreak of the disease." Both of the sons died. The woman was the very picture of grief, always dressed in black, à la Eleonora Duse, always wandering restlessly about the garden. She could just speak a little French, and she spoke the same words to whomever she saw: "Vous savez, tous les dé." That was "Tous les deux."

Then the directress with the sty—now what was her name? In the book she is called "Adriatica von Mylendonk." She had such a noble name. And "Jessen" himself, with his oil painting; also the girl with the whistling pneumothorax, "Hermine Kleefeld"—that was her real name, I believe—and Fräulein "Levi," that other member of the "Half-Lung Club." I also told him about the one who "died very respectably."

"Herr Albin," however, was in Arosa—"Herr Albin," who was always so boastful, always fumbling with his revolver and threatening to shoot himself, who also passed around and devoured so many chocolates. Many other characters in the novel came from Arosa too.

I intentionally wrote down little details for my husband because I knew he was working on the book. He began it right after his first visit to Davos, and by the time I was in Arosa he had already written a great deal. There were many particulars in the letters, which have all been lost. It would be grist for the Germanists' mills to compare those letters with *The Magic Mountain*, but they can't do that now, and it doesn't make any difference either. The Germanists do far too much comparing as it is.

In Davos there was a Madame Chauchat, who always slammed the door. At first, she really did get on my husband's nerves a great deal, but later he became very sensitive to her charm. This woman, a Slavic-Russian patient, must also have reminded him of that Slavic boy, Pribislav Hippe, who had once been his schoolmate.

The story about Pribislav and the pencil in the schoolyard certainly did take place; a reminiscence, no doubt, which the woman had awakened in my husband. But on the other hand, he never returned a pencil to *her* —that was Hans Castorp. Thomas Mann's feeling for Madame Chauchat didn't go that far; after all, he was there to visit *me*. He merely observed her and found her pleasing. He didn't wait for her any seven years either, nor did he carry on with her in the Walpurgis Night, which is purely imaginary, since he visited me in the summer, in June.

It is also a fact that Jessen examined him and immediately said, "You have a spot on one of your lungs and would do well to remain here for six months with your wife." My husband reported this to our family doctor in Munich, who then wrote back: "I know you very well. You would be the first one to be examined in Davos who did *not* have some spot or other. Return to Munich immediately. You have no business in Davos."

The story about the streptococci is also true. Jessen actually couldn't explain why I always had a temperature, even though my cure was progressing so well. He took some blood and made a culture; then he came and said, "They're streptococci!" But I think that was all nonsense.

My husband knew Settembrini from somewhere else; and the psychoanalyst who gave the series of lectures on "love as a force contributory to disease" wasn't there either. That was invented. In the psychoanalyst Krokowski's case, Thomas Mann was thinking partly of Dr. Bircher in Zurich. There was also an assistant in Davos by the name of Müller, but he was completely different.

There was no Naphta either. Leo Naphta, as he appears in the novel, is pure fiction. But in 1922 we were in Vienna, staying at the Hotel Imperial, and Georg Lukács visited us there. He was living in exile because he had been mixed up in the Hungarian revolt of 1919 under Béla Kun. He started right in with the development of his theories, lecturing at us for a whole hour in our room. My husband couldn't get a word in; he just got to say, "Yes, yes, very interesting." Then Lukács was gone.

That was all he knew of Lukács at that time. Later Lukács wrote a very nice, intelligent book about Thomas Mann; but my husband saw and listened to him only this once in his life. He never spoke of Lukács again, and never thought about him.

When he read me the chapter about Naphta, with the description of his appearance, I asked, "Were you thinking of Lukács there?"

"No, why?"

"I don't know. Naphta reminds me of him."

"It was quite unintentional, but it may be that Lukács was at the back of my mind."

Naturally, it is only Naphta's appearance and his

gift for lecturing without interruption that are reminiscent of him. He had seen and heard him for no more than an hour. But that was the remarkable thing about him: he got a complete picture of a person immediately. He studied Lukács as a model as little as he did Holitscher; he didn't follow Lukács with opera glasses either. He didn't observe people for the sake of portraying them afterward. Once he had seen someone, he had a mental image of him, and when a fictional figure came along whom this someone matched, the someone popped up again, but not intentionally. There is no question of that. That's the way it was with the Krull family. Asked about his models, Thomas Mann answered, "Oh, I once watched them for half an hour on a Rhine steamer."

One anecdote indicates his powers of memory, although he never portrayed the family seamstress in a book. During the time when all six children were at home, we had a large dining-room table in Munich. My husband sat at one end, I sat next to him, across from me perhaps Erika, then came the other children, and at the other end sat the two little ones and the governess. Every two weeks a so-called family seamstress, a Fräulein Rössner, joined us. My husband sat at some distance from her, since the table was long. Now, this Fräulein came for several years, and then she stopped coming. She was the niece of good friends in Zurich. Once we visited these friends, the Reiffs, and met Fräulein Rössner there. My husband immediately greeted her and said, "Oh, Fräulein Rössner, it's nice to see you again! Where is your ring with the little diamond? And you're wearing a pince-nez and not your regular glasses." The woman must have thought he had always been watching her and had perhaps had ulterior motives as well. He simply looked at her, without any designs on her and without any particular interest. In this respect, he was a complete "eye" type and, as far as impressionability goes, was just like Hans Castorp. My husband, however, was not as ingenuous as Castorp; the characterization "life's problem child" couldn't be applied to him either, although he did give Hans Castorp many of his own traits. Castorp is something of a self-portrait, only simplified. All of Thomas Mann's subjective figures, including Joseph and Krull, represent some form of the artist—both this particular artist and the artist in general—and Hans Castorp was simply his ingenuous side, but at the same time a side very open to impressions.

The Magic Mountain aroused hostility among the people of Davos because it gave the impression that young people from wealthy families, captivated by the atmosphere of the sanatorium and by the amenities of that form of existence, were kept there when they were no longer ill because of the profit motive and the licentiousness of the place. Sometimes the Hofrat speaks of the sanatorium as though it were a pleasure palace, and the laxity was tremendous: one could go from one room to another by way of the balconies—morally speaking, things were certainly not beyond reproach up there. Naturally, a stay in a sanatorium was also very beneficial for many patients.

And Jessen! In my opinion Jessen is the most sympathetic figure in *The Magic Mountain;* he is basically a kind and nice man in the book. He's very unusual, and that's the way he really was. He had a funny way of being flippant. And it is really true that he said to a dying patient, little Barbara Hujus, "Don't behave like that!" And that she indeed then "died very respectably." Many people find him, along with Peeperkorn, the most sympathetic figure in the novel. But in his own view he had grounds for complaint. Later he got over it, though.

Many years later we sent a check to one of his sons, who had been in the First World War and had taken part in the mutiny of the fleet. Things were not going well for him, and a well-meaning friend was collecting money for him. But he didn't want the check, was annoyed, and returned the money. Accompanying it was a note: "I know it was well meant, but it was very foolish of my friend, for my situation is not that bad; please don't think I am returning the check because you used my father as a model for *The Magic Mountain*. I don't hold that against you."

Today Davos has changed completely. All the sanatoriums are now resort hotels. When I was in Klosters last year, the citizens of Davos insisted on giving me a party in honor of *The Magic Mountain*. Well, they went ahead with it, and the party wasn't without its comic side, when you think of all the bad feeling there once had been. Now they are very proud of the book.

I can't say exactly how far Thomas Mann had progressed in the writing of *The Magic Mountain* when he began his *Reflections*. During the war he was so caught up by his political and nationalistic emotions that it was impossible for him to continue work on the novel. Thus, it was interrupted by the *Reflections*, and not until after the war did he again turn to the world of fiction in his two idylls, "A Man and His Dog" and "Song of the Child." Then in 1919 he returned to *The Magic Mountain*. But he thought it was a good thing that he had written the *Reflections*, for otherwise *The Magic Mountain* would have been much too weighed down with political and philosophical concerns, and he would never have introduced a figure like Settembrini. To that extent, the novel is indebted to the *Reflections*.

Thomas Mann wrote very slowly, but what he wrote was final; he changed virtually nothing. He always made elaborate preparations for his writing. Whereas Heinrich sometimes wrote in the evenings too, my husband never did. The only thing he ever wrote in the evening (also after a drink or two) is "The Wardrobe." Otherwise he wrote only in the morning. He could work only when his head was completely clear. His daily schedule was very disciplined, simple, and always took the same course. He wrote approximately from nine until twelve, then he took a walk, ate lunch, read the paper in the afternoon, smoked a cigar, and took a nap. After tea he took another walk, read and took notes on the reading he did for his writing, and took care of what he called "the demands of the day." Only those three morning hours were set aside for his creative work. He wrote everything by hand, and if he wrote two pages in one day, it was more than usual.

Apropos writing by hand: after he had finished *Buddenbrooks,* he sealed the manuscript without its being copied, burned himself badly while doing so, and took it to the post office. Then he told the postal clerk he wanted to have the package insured—it was a manuscript.

The clerk replied, "Well, well. You want to insure it? For how much? Hmmm?"

"For a thousand marks, I think."

The clerk (with great surprise): "What? One thousand marks? Well, whatever you say."

That was the launching of *Buddenbrooks.*

My husband did not discuss the technical aspects of his work with me. Occasionally he let me in on his plans—things which he would perhaps someday write. But until the time of *The Magic Mountain,* when I was well acquainted with the subject matter and could advise him, I never did so directly. That would have been a mistake. I did not collaborate on his books.

He often couldn't share his intentions with me because he was unclear about them himself. As I have said, he never planned a Joseph tetralogy. When the work kept getting longer and longer, he said he had no idea when and in what form to have it published. Then I made a suggestion: "Heavens, I would have it published in installments. I wouldn't wait until this endless task is over. I would simply bring out the first volume. It's just impossible," I said, "to have nothing appear for years and then suddenly this gigantic work. It can be broken up, can't it?" That is what he subsequently did. *The Tales of Jacob* as the first volume, then *Young*

Joseph, and so on. Perhaps he wouldn't have done it that way if his clever wife hadn't suggested it. Perhaps he wouldn't even have begun *Joseph* if he had known that he would be working on it for so many years.

When he had concluded the tetralogy, the next thing he wrote was *The Tables of the Law*, and then he planned to do something on a large scale again. He had the idea either of continuing *Krull* or of writing something which would encompass the whole epoch of decline which finally degenerated into National Socialism. He had broken off work on *Krull* because he didn't believe he could sustain its parodistic tone throughout the whole book. I strongly urged him not to go back to *Krull* yet, but to write *Faustus* instead. "You know," I said, "*Joseph* of course has relevance for the present day, yet you might say it's somewhat escapist too. If you continue with *Krull* now, that tendency will become even stronger. I think it's better to pursue the *Faustus* plan." And that's what he did.

Later he enjoyed working on *Krull*. After having dropped it for four decades, he found the right tone again when he returned to it in 1951. The point of resumption is not noticeable at all. He had a lot of fun with *The Holy Sinner* too. While he was still working on *Faustus*, in which the Gregorius legend with its double incest appears, he said, "I'm going to do that; I'm going to take it away from Adrian Leverkühn."

I heard everything for the first time when he read it aloud. He would read a chapter at a time. When he had finished a section, he read it to me and later also to the children at family gatherings. He liked that very much, for he found it stimulating to hear what he had written and to observe the effect it had on others. No one else could read his things as well as he. He was also receptive to minor criticism: you could call his attention to details or little inconsistencies. "Perhaps that's not quite right. . . ." "Well, I'll think it over; yes, maybe I'll change that." These readings were a kind of rehearsal for him. He never read what he had written that very day, and he rarely read aloud anything other than what he himself had written. Naturally, this did happen on occasion if there was a special reason. One book he liked to read aloud, *When Grandfather Married Grandmother*, was a collection of ballads and moralizing poems. In its way a precursor of *Struwwelpeter*, it contained little verses such as this:

> *His sweet tooth was the death of him;*
> *The cup he thought was sugar*
> *Was arsenic to the brim.*

My husband knew many poems by heart. (Golo inherited this from him; he too has an incredible store of poetry in his head.) Above all, my husband knew many poems by Platen and Goethe, and when the occasion arose, he loved to quote them.

If my husband was not yet sure about a particular scene, was depressed and worried about how to handle it, he sometimes didn't keep his problem to himself until it was solved, but discussed it with me. Then he would come and say something like, "I'm not quite clear about it yet. . . ." I would listen to him and say,

"But what do you mean? I would imagine that. . . ."
I very rarely gave him inspiration for his books. Regarding particular worries which he had and which I
knew about, I can only remember one conversation
about a very late story, *The Black Swan*. It had to do
with the point at which Rosalie von Thümmler learns
of her illness. I said to him, "It must come very late in
the story. It's completely out of the question that she
have any inkling of it earlier." *The Black Swan* is not
one of his major works, and many people don't like it.
They find it unsavory. I, on the other hand, like it. I
find it stylistically interesting because of the rather old-
fashioned tone of narration. Also, the relationship between the mother and daughter seems to me to be done
very successfully. By the way, although I very seldom
gave him ideas for his work, in this case I did inspire
the story. We had an acquaintance, who—like Frau von
Thümmler—was getting on in years but had not reached
the menopause. Once when we were talking about her,
I said, "That worries me a little. It could be something
pathological."

"How do you mean?"

"I once knew a woman, Frau So-and-so. She was
in love with a younger man. One day she came triumphantly to tell me her secret: 'Just imagine! I've begun menstruating again.' It turned out to be cancer of
the uterus."

My husband was very impressed by this. "You
know, it's fascinating. It's so striking that I'm going to
have to do something with it."

We thought alike about so many things. After all, I was married to the man for fifty years.

Interjections from Outside

E.M.: Clearly, for us children there were always these two figures side by side: the father, the husband, the man of the house, the human being close to us; and the literary figure projected toward the outside world, the figure of the artist Thomas Mann, whose influence reached further and further as time went on.

G.M.: In the home of a writer like my father, reality is confusing to a certain extent: the realm of art and the realm of reality, or so-called reality, get mixed up in a peculiar way. For example, we children naturally read the novel *Buddenbrooks* at an early age and later became very familiar with it. Now, as for what is really family history in it and what belongs to the sphere of art—there was practically no dividing line between the two for us, nor can one be clearly drawn. When I was a young man, I once visited the grave of my grandfather in Lübeck, in other words, of the Senator in *Buddenbrooks*. And as I was standing there in front of the imposing gravestone with its coat of arms and "Senator Heinrich Mann" and so forth, I had the distinct feeling that I was really standing in front of the gravestone of Thomas Buddenbrook, you know what I mean? To what extent the two figures are truly similar, how exact the portrait is, I can't judge.

E.M.: Thomas Buddenbrook, usually believed to be simply a portrait—or not simply, but still more or less a portrait—of Senator Mann, my father's father, of course isn't after all. That's the way it is in novels—everything is all mixed up; that is to say, there is a great deal of Thomas Mann in each of the figures in *Buddenbrooks,* especially in Thomas but also in Christian and also in Tony, and in all the figures more or less. And we learned how to keep them apart at a relatively early age. The Mann family history concerned us less; the book concerned us more.

The figure of my father's mother in *Buddenbrooks* was not a true portrait either. Gerda was a fictional character, almost entirely fictional, like Tonio Kröger's very vaguely sketched mother. But his own mother he "spared," I might almost say. He was very attached to her, and strangely enough, in this particular case it would have gone against his grain to use her as a model. T.M. did only one sketch, "Portrait of My Mother" (the title isn't even his), in which he describes his mother the way he saw her as a boy, a stylized portrait, not really very lifelike, stereotyped, not at all detailed, a little romanticized. The only time she appears in a novel approximately the way she was in life is in a minor role in *Dr. Faustus*—as the mother of the two Rodde sisters, but although the role is small, she stands out as a distinct personality. And she had already been dead for a long time by then. In general, T.M. did things in *Faustus* which he himself referred to as ruthless.

When I read *Royal Highness* for the first time, I was well aware that the book—particularly in the beginning when the prince is courting Imma—coincides to a large extent with my parents' own story, in a stylized way. I also knew that when my father was writing the book, he borrowed the letters he had written my mother during their courtship, and that he made some use of parts of them—the whole thing is a remarkable blending. One is perfectly able to approach the purely personal part of it with curiosity and pride, to appreciate and enjoy it, and to confront the book as such, as a work of art, as a novel, as a creation by one's father, to read it with suspense and try to figure out what's purely fictional and what's based on reality. The two belong side by side, and they always have.

I don't recognize my mother directly in any figures other than Imma and Rachel. In the case of us children, naturally my sister Elisabeth is the child in "Song of the Child" and is clearly recognizable in *Disorder and Early Sorrow*. Klaus and I also appear to a certain extent in the latter work; the middle two—the so-called "middle ones," as opposed to "the big ones" and "the little ones"—were left out. So my brother Golo and my sister Monika are omitted. As far as Klaus and I are concerned —it's quite a business with so-called models and roman-à-clef figures. Quite naturally, he made a kind of hash out of our characteristics, even our outward ones. He made us older in the story than we really were at the time. In reality, we were at the most fourteen and fifteen, I should say; so in actual fact our childish behavior occurred at an earlier point in our lives than in the lives of the children in *Disorder*. It is a humorous story. T.M. was much more aware of the difficulties of young people and of our own difficulties in particular than is evident in it. These young people, these adolescents, were important accessories, but the story really revolves around the little girl, the milieu, and the figure of Professor Abel Cornelius, in whom T.M. is reflected, but again only in a very indirectly autobiographical way, and only to a certain extent; it really revolves around the unhappiness of being in love, the disorder and the early sorrow—without anyone being able to say: Here is this or that real person.

As for the portrait of a city as background in the novellas—if the city isn't named, it's just as it was with the characters: there isn't any one key. Naturally Lübeck often appears in a partial, fragmentary way. Of course, every poet and every artist remains the prisoner of his childhood to a certain extent, else he wouldn't be a poet or an artist. T.M. turned back to his own past in *Dr. Faustus* by returning to the atmosphere of the German medieval towns. The town of Kaisersaschern bears a strong resemblance to Lübeck, and he really felt that he had drawn a full circle from *Faustus* back to *Buddenbrooks. Felix Krull,* which he resumed work on forty years after he had begun it, also represents the completion of a circle, although in a quite different way.

VII

As CHANCE OR FATE would have it, we went abroad on a lecture tour in February 1933. We didn't return to Germany from this trip; of necessity it led us into exile. That is why we didn't emigrate in the literal meaning of the word, for fortunately we were already "away." We would never have been able to emigrate.

For months I had been saying to my husband, "The Nazis are going to take over: nothing can stop them now. And the way you have always attacked them puts us in a terribly dangerous situation. It would be better for us to leave the country." But he always said, "I won't do that. It would be a signal that I believe in the victory of their cause, and that's a signal I don't want to give. We'll just stay where we are; for the time being nothing will happen to us."

The Nazi boycott was flagrant by 1930, and Thomas Mann had already found out by then how obviously unpopular he was in certain circles. In October 1930 he gave a talk, "German Address: An Appeal to Reason," in the Beethoven Hall in Berlin. He went there with the express purpose of using that platform to warn against the Nazis, to speak out against them. That evening, with all the commotion and excitement it brought, is one I'll never forget. The hall was half-filled with a friendly audience, but up in the gallery sat Herr Arnolt Bronnen with some like-minded companions—pro-Nazi, aggressive—hoping to stop the speech. They made a terrible racket, continually interrupting my husband with: "Nonsense!" "Enough!" and the like, so that he had to break off for a while. There was tremendous unrest in the hall. Then practically the entire audience turned toward the gallery and cried, "We want to hear Thomas Mann. Quiet up there!" He was able to continue without much further disturbance. I was sitting in the first row; Frau Fischer was sitting on the podium, and she kept whispering, "Finish quickly. Finish as soon as possible." But my husband was not to be deterred, and he continued to the very end.

Afterward Bruno Walter came to us in the green room and said, "You know, I wouldn't go out by the main stairway now. You never know what might happen. I know my way around here. I'll take you down the back stairs." And that's what he did. We got out that way, by means of a few connecting passageways; then Bruno Walter took us to his car, which he had parked in a courtyard, and got us away safely.

The next day a picture that was meant to be an attack appeared in an illustrated Nazi paper, showing the gathering in the Beethoven Hall. When the audience had turned to the gallery to demand silence, a photographer had snapped a picture of all the people turning their backs on the speaker; the caption read: "Thomas Mann gives a speech." From that moment he was officially identified as an enemy of the Nazis.

ABOVE LEFT, *Katia, April 1886.* ABOVE RIGHT, *Katia and her twin brother, Klaus Pringsheim, April 1885.* BELOW, *The five Pringsheim children: Peter, Heinz, Klaus, Erik, and Katia (on pedestal), April 1886*

Children's Carnival: Four Pierrots and a Pierrette, *the Pringsheim children, 1889*

Hedwig Pringsheim and her children, Arci-strasse, Munich, 1891; (reading from top) *Peter, Erik, Klaus, Katia, and Heinz*

Katia with her mother, 1889–90

Katia, April 1887

Katia, 1893

Katia, 1899　　　　　　*Katia, 1892*

Klaus and Katia, ready to enter university, 1900

Katia with her son Klaus on the veranda, Arci-strasse, Munich, 1907

*Katia and her children at their home in Munich,
September 1919: Erika, Elisabeth, Klaus, Katia,
Michael, Golo, and Monika*

LEFT, *Katia with Erika and Klaus, 1907.*   RIGHT,
*Katia with Golo in her arms, Erika, Thomas, and
Klaus; Tölz, 1909*

On Alfred Pringsheim's eightieth birthday at the
Manns' vacation home, Nidden, September 2,
1930: Elisabeth, Golo, Katia, Alfred and Hedwig
Pringsheim, and Thomas

Katia, Elisabeth, and Arthur Nikisch (son of the
famous conductor). Arosa, Winter 1933

Thomas and Katia. Nidden, Summer 1930

Golo, Mrs. René Schickele, Mrs. Julius Meier-Graefe, Thomas, Julius Meier-Graefe, Katia, her cousin Ilse Dernberg, and Erika. Sanary, 1933

Katia and her son Klaus, 1927

Thomas and Katia. New York, April 1937

*Else and Bruno Walter with Katia. Pacific
Palisades, 1943*

Katia and Thomas with their grandsons Frido and Tonio. Pacific Palisades, 1948

On Thomas Mann's seventy-fifth birthday,
Zurich, June 6, 1950: Gret (Mrs. Michael Mann),
Thomas, Katia, Erika, Elisabeth, and Michael

Katia with Frido and Tonio. Erlenbach, 1953

Thomas and Katia in their garden. Kilchberg-
Zurich, 1955

Katia. Zurich, 1966

Katia in her garden. Kilchberg-Zurich, 1971

We had a summer house in Nidden for a short time, and we spent the summer of '32, our last summer in Germany, up there by the sea. During that time the murders took place in Potempa. It must have been the end of July or the beginning of August. In Potempa (in Silesia, I believe) there had been violent disagreement between Social Democrat and National Socialist workers, and the Nazis had stamped the Social Democrats' throats under their heels. They murdered them brutally like that. Hitler couldn't think of any way to respond to this crime—and what else was to be expected of him? —except to send the murderers a congratulatory telegram in which he referred to them as his comrades and pledged them his eternal loyalty. These "comrades," naturally, were not arrested.

The *Berliner Tageblatt* called us up and said something had to be done about it. My husband sat down and wrote a furious article with the headline "What We Must Demand" and sent it to the *Berliner Tageblatt*. In it he took a strong stand against the Nazis, their murderous excesses and accusations. But the paper called up a second time: "We can't print your article exactly as it stands. The Nazis would burn the building. We'll have to tone it down a bit, and then we'll be glad to publish it."

Our house in Nidden had a very pretty setting, with a view of the lagoon, and woods out back. Every morning we took a walk in the woods before breakfast, and we hardly ever saw anyone. If we did, it was someone wearing linen trousers, dressed in vacation clothes for the country—in short, in a summer suit. But one day—it was after the business of these murders—I saw some people in city clothes walking in the woods, and I said to my husband, "That's funny, what are they doing here?" We soon turned around and went back home. They followed us into our yard. I—really like Leonore in *Fidelio*—stood in front of my husband and said harshly to them, "What do you want here?" They replied, "Mais, Madame, nous sommes des journalistes belges, nous avons entendu votre mari à Bruxelles et nous voulons un petit interview."

I said, "Alors, très bien."

Well and good, but in those days one really had to be prepared for the worst. The Nazis had already committed several political murders.

A short time later Thomas Mann addressed an assembly of workers in Vienna, attacking the Nazis. Then he was called upon to speak in Berlin at a gathering of the Socialist Kulturbund. This meeting never took place; it was banned by the Nazis after they seized power. It was barely possible to print Thomas Mann's speech, "An Avowal of Socialism," in a Socialist periodical.

He did what he could. Heinrich always was far to the left, as people knew. But Thomas Mann was the only one of the so-called bourgeois writers to speak out against the Nazis. Not one of them, neither Hermann Stehr nor Gerhart Hauptmann, or anyone else, stood up against them. My husband seemed to be the only one.

Then came the lecture tour, from which we were never to return. Thomas Mann had been invited to lecture on Richard Wagner on the occasion of the fiftieth anniversary of his death: in German in Amsterdam, in

French in Brussels and Paris. Before we left the country, my husband began the series with "Sufferings and Greatness of Richard Wagner" on February 10, 1933, in the Grand Auditorium of the University of Munich. The lecture was sold out, it was quite well received, and a very fair and positive review appeared in the Munich newspaper, *Neueste Nachrichten*. The next day we left for Holland. I remember the date exactly because it is also our wedding anniversary.

In order to rest a little after the Wagner tour, we went to Arosa. While we were there, the burning of the Reichstag took place on February 27. Then came the National Assembly elections of March 5, by which time all the Communists and many of the Social Democrats were already behind bars. Everybody in the hotel gathered around the radio to hear the election results. I was sitting by the radio with my daughter Medi (Elisabeth), and I kept saying, "It's absolutely ridiculous. You can't call that a free election. They've locked up most of the opposition. What can come of it?"

Then someone said, "Madam, be careful what you say."

"I don't have to be careful," I said. "We can't go back in any case."

And we couldn't. It would have been completely out of the question, but my husband still didn't quite believe it.

We called up Erika and Klaus, who were in Munich. Being sure they would understand what I really meant, I said, "I don't know, but don't you think that this would be the time for a spring cleaning?"

(what I was asking them, of course, was whether they considered it advisable for us to return home). But Erika said, "No, no, and besides the weather is terrible. Just stay there for a little while; you're not missing a thing." After this conversation it was perfectly clear that we had to remain outside the country with the few things we had with us—we had taken nothing but the necessities for a three-week trip.

My husband still had vague hopes of returning. But then in April a stupid article, "Protest of the Richard-Wagner-City of Munich," appeared in the Munich *Neueste Nachrichten*. It was directed against his lecture "Sufferings and Greatness of Richard Wagner," which had initially been so very favorably received. Meanwhile the Nazis had come to power, and this "protest" in Munich was only one sign of the direction things were taking.

My husband's piece was a psychologically oriented essay which gave a portrait of Wagner as an ambiguous and remarkable figure with his great gifts as well as his human weaknesses and peculiarities. It showed Thomas Mann's great involvement with Wagner's work. Thus, the "protest" made no sense at all.

My husband was more or less under the influence of Richard Wagner his whole life long, especially as a young man, and he never missed a *Tristan* performance. In his middle years he distanced himself from Wagner somewhat, but he never freed himself entirely. There is an anecdote I always like to tell: it was when we went to Italy in 1953 and saw a fine performance of *Otello*. When we were home again—we were living in Erlenbach near Zurich—he said, "Oh, put on the record with the entr'acte music from *Parsifal*." He loved hearing it, and when the record was over, he said, "Yes, the *Otello* we heard recently was very good, but when I hear *this*, ach, du lieber Gott!" That's the way it was until the end of his life.

He also learned the whole "leitmotif" technique from Wagner, although he had found anticipations of it in Zola (as well as in Tolstoy).

But back to the "Protest of the Richard-Wagner-City of Munich," which everyone who was anyone in Munich had signed: the Bavarian cultural minister, the president of the Academy of Fine Arts, Clemens von Franckenstein—who was the director of the Bavarian Staatstheater—Gulbransson, Pfitzner, Richard Strauss, Knappertsbusch, and I don't know who else. They found it shocking that my husband had given the speech abroad. Among other things the protest contained the sentence: "We will not permit the solid value of our intellectual giant to be undermined abroad by a Thomas Mann"—solid value, as though it were a matter of a gilt-edged security. It was a terribly polemical article against him, and it upset him out of all proportion. My father flew into a rage, which he tended to do by nature. In bewilderment he asked, "But how is it possible? The essay begins in this vein: 'A passion for Richard Wagner permeates my life!' Such love and such knowledge of Wagner's works are there in every sentence. . . . It's a disgrace for these people to write such a thing." At moments like this, his coolness toward his son-in-law vanished; he became furious on his behalf, fought for him, helped him.

In response to the "Protest," Bermann Fischer published a questionnaire in the *Rundschau* to find out people's reasons for signing the statement. There were some peculiar answers. For example, Gulbransson wrote, "You know, I wasn't even aware of the wording. But everyone signed it. A man I admire very much, and his wife—" That was all he could say.

The way things stood, Thomas Mann would not have been able to return in any case unless he had declared that he had misinterpreted the situation and now realized that what was at stake was after all a renewal of Germany. Then he would have been taken in again and highly honored by the new Knights of the Grail. They even approached him about returning. In the case of Richard Strauss, the Wagner affair had a brief epilogue. We knew Strauss quite well. I had already met him in my parents' home, and when my twin brother was a young musician, he respected him highly. Now, our friends the Reiffs lived in Zurich. My husband even portrayed them by name in *Dr. Faustus*. It was a part of the technique of that novel that such borrowings from reality occurred in it from time to time. Frau Reiff was, I believe, the last pupil of Liszt, and she was very eager to have all musicians who came to Zurich and performed there stay in her house. She had a big, beautiful home, and Strauss was a guest there shortly after the Nazi seizure of power. There was much talk about Thomas Mann, and Strauss exclaimed, "Ah, I would like to see him again some time."

Frau Reiff called us up. "Would you be willing to come to our house for lunch tomorrow with Strauss?" My husband declined: "Oh, I'd rather not."

This she reported to Strauss: "Thomas Mann doesn't care to come."

"What? Ach. Because of that silly business a while ago?"

He called the protest "that silly business"! We never saw him again.

First we stayed in Switzerland, but then we went to southern France, to Sanary-sur-Mer, where friends had found a house for us. During the first months of our exile my husband was often so agitated or depressed that he was unable to write at all. There was no guarantee of a secure future, and the thought of an exile lasting for years, maybe even for the rest of his life, preyed upon his mind. As a good German, he felt himself much too closely connected with the German language, with the German cultural heritage, to be able to face this new existence without the greatest reservations. But gradually he regained his composure and also began to write again. He was working on *Joseph* then. We had our youngest children with us, and a whole circle of German emigrants had gathered in Sanary. Heinrich was there, as well as Julius Meier-Graefe, a prominent man, intelligent and nice; René Schickele and the Feuchtwangers were living there too. We knew Lion Feuchtwanger very well, although we had only seen him occasionally in Germany because he lived in Berlin. In fact, I had already known him in school, the Wilhelms-Gymnasium in Munich, when I was sitting my Abitur. And Thomas Mann was on especially good terms with him, also later in California, where we visited them. At Christmas and on other occasions, they also often visited us in our house in Pacific Palisades. Feuchtwanger was very intelligent and most amusing. He was quite vain, but in a completely disarming way. I remember he told me once in Sanary that some book or other of his was about to appear simultaneously in French, Italian, and Spanish— only the American version naturally wouldn't be ready until later because he always had to mail the manuscript, and then the galley proofs, all that way. So I said, "Heavens, Herr Feuchtwanger, I really can't understand why you put up with that. Why didn't you telegraph the manuscript to America?"

"Ach, I never thought of that." He didn't even notice that I was making fun of him.

Thomas Mann liked his books. They really were written with great knowledge of the subject matter, and several were excellent in their way, especially the later ones, *Goya* and *The Jewess of Toledo*.

We were very friendly with René Schickele, and often got together with him. He was a delightful, amiable man, had a good sense of humor, and was intelligent. We three—he, his wife, and I—were all the same age, and we celebrated his fiftieth birthday in Sanary. While we were eating, someone said, "Oh, what a fine party we'd be having now in Berlin, if we could have celebrated your birthday there." I said quite simply, "The company couldn't have been any better there."

Once Valéry came to visit, and we spoke French together, which I could do very well, and I said, "Hitler is simply anti-intellectual. More than anything else, he

would like to do away with intellect entirely." Whereupon Valéry replied, "Come to think of it, that's a good
idea."

"Yes, but you can entertain that idea only if you
possess intellect yourself."

"That's good, that's excellent," he said, highly delighted.

From France my husband was drawn back to
Switzerland, for which he had always had a special
fondness. We also wanted to move to a German-
speaking area for the sake of the youngest children, who
were still in school. First we thought of Basel, but that
plan fell through, and so we rented a house in Küsnacht
near Zurich, where we remained for five years. Some
upsetting things happened there, but in general life was
quite pleasant for us. In the beginning Thomas Mann
had been hesitant to make a complete break with Germany; he was eager that his books still be read there
because he thought this fact alone would keep many
people from throwing themselves into the arms of
Fascism. But he soon realized that this was not possible,
that he would be misrepresented and described as not
having left Germany in protest at all, which would
only cause confusion and was irresponsible nonsense.
Finally he wrote a reply to Eduard Korrodi, the literary
editor of the *Neue Zürcher Zeitung*, who, in his article
"German Literature in the Mirror of the Emigrants,"
had equated emigrant literature with "the Jewish novel
industry." In his "Open Letter to Korrodi" my husband
corrected the assertions made in the article and declared
himself to be unequivocally on the side of the emigrants,

thus drawing the final line of separation between Germany and himself. At that point we lost our German citizenship.

It did not come to a break with Korrodi; he admired my husband, and I don't think he took his response amiss. Besides, the "Open Letter" was directed at Germany. In regard to the ideas and expectations current in Germany, it was necessary for Thomas Mann to clarify his relationship to the Third Reich with a radical rejection of this sort.

When we returned to Zurich for the first time after the war, in 1947, for a P.E.N. Congress, Korrodi was still alive, and we went with him on a horse-and-wagon outing he had organized to the Untersee. He held no grudges against my husband.

In the Küsnacht period Thomas Mann continued work on the *Joseph* novels, which he personally considered his favorite, best, most substantive and significant work. Surprisingly, in the whole tetralogy he used no models. Except for Mai-Sachme (who was our friend Martin Gumpert, a doctor and a writer), the many figures are all fictional, including Laban, for example, which you might not expect. It has often been said that in describing Rachel my husband was thinking of me. She is so spirited, and the way she steals the teraphim, her clandestine actions—maybe there is something to it. To be sure, I didn't die in childbirth, but I could have. Thomas Mann described that scene with great feeling.

At times he thought Adrian Leverkühn in *Faustus* was his favorite character, but ultimately he rated

Joseph highest, as the prototype of the artist, a figure he treated in very diverse forms.

During those years the three older children were already grown up and no longer living at home. Klaus was in Holland, editing the magazine *Die Sammlung*, which he had founded with Heinrich, Gide, and Huxley. Golo had found a position as teacher in a school in St. Cloud, and Erika had her cabaret. Her marriage to Gründgens had ended long before. Gustaf Gründgens had always been very inhibited when he visited us in Munich, first as fiancé, then later as a married man in a bourgeois family—roles that didn't suit him at all. Incidentally, the actor Herzl in the novella *Disorder and Early Sorrow* is definitely not Gründgens. Rather, the model my husband had in mind was a young matinee idol from Munich named Albert Fischel, whom my adolescent children admired very much. We didn't yet know Gründgens at that time. Fischel was very handsome and still quite young. He played the role of Don Carlos, and he said, "My Carlos is all of a piece," just as Herzl does in the story.

Erika had been able to open "The Pepper Mill" in Munich to great acclaim, although it was shortly before the Nazi takeover. Later she continued the cabaret in Switzerland, beginning in Zurich. Naturally, I saw several programs, including the premiere performance in Munich. She really did it extremely well. She and Therese Giehse were the pillars of the undertaking.

In other countries as well, above all in Holland and Czechoslovakia, they experienced tremendous success. When my husband and I went to Holland in 1955, all the Dutchmen we met immediately spoke of it, "Ah, 'The Pepper Mill' in those days. That was really something unique!" Therese Giehse frequently visited us in Küsnacht. She was a friend of Erika's and became a close friend of the family; when they returned to Zurich from their tours, she stayed with us. She was always there for Christmas and was a part of things. Aside from her great talent, she is warm-hearted and natural. She is very Jewish, but at the same time Bavarian through and through, and Hitler was especially taken with her. He saw in her an artist of the Volk, such as you find only in Germany. When one of his cronies pointed out that the lady was not a pure Aryan, he declared that such a view was malicious gossip; he, Hitler, could tell with unfailing judgment what was natural Germanic talent and what was Semitic sham.

In a performance of a play by Klaus entitled *The Siblings* and reminiscent of Cocteau's *Enfants Terribles*, Therese portrayed a good-hearted cook in the household of the children, these "enfants terribles." The play itself caused a scandal and aroused great hostility on the part of the critics. Therese alone was praised: after all this dissolute youth, they said, it was a relief to see an authentically Bavarian, natural woman like Frau Giehse in the role of the cook. She was extraordinarily Bavarian —as was Feuchtwanger, by the way.

Erika and Klaus—as well as "the middle ones," Monika and Golo—always came to visit us; the youngest children were still at home. Elisabeth went to the Freie Gymnasium in Zurich and was such a good student that she graduated at seventeen. I was at the graduation ceremony, and the principal handed each student his diploma; when he got to Elisabeth he said, "This student made such good use of her time that we can't give her her diploma yet because she is not allowed to enter the university until she is eighteen years old. On her eighteenth birthday the diploma will be mailed to her."

Michael wanted to be a musician and went to the Zurich Conservatory, where he studied the violin. First he received his teaching diploma, and then he was supposed to get a concert diploma in addition. But an encounter with the director of the Conservatory put an end to that. This man, who was most unpleasant, was hated by all the teachers. Michael, who sometimes went into a practice room during a break to play the piano, had a revolting experience with him. The director came in one day while Michael was playing and demanded, "What are you doing here?"

"I thought during the break . . ."

"But you know that's forbidden!"

Saying this, he grabbed Michael by the shoulder, whereupon Michael gave the man a box on the ear and was immediately expelled. All the professors congratulated him because someone had finally given this director his due; but Michael's act of self-defense ended with his hasty exit and without his having the second diploma in his pocket. He continued his study of the violin, and then came to America to join us.

Erika had succeeded in reaching Munich after the takeover and getting the *Joseph* manuscript, along with a few other manuscripts, out of our house, which had already been confiscated. But the rest—all the manuscripts from *Buddenbrooks* and the early novellas on, all the correspondence, my husband's letters as well as letters from Hofmannsthal and others which I had saved—were lost as a result of our emigration.

I had piles of letters from my husband, for during our time in Munich we had often been separated on account of his lecture tours, and he always wrote me at length on these trips. During the periods of my illnesses, when I had to go to the mountains for my health, he wrote me twice a week: long reports about the family, himself, and what he was doing. If they were still extant, they would provide a kind of biography for that period.

I had a friend in Munich who was not very well off, and I offered her daughter the job of arranging all my letters so that she could earn some money. Little Dora was the dearest girl; she came once a week, ate lunch with us, and then put the letters in chronological order, a folder for each year. That was how I gave them to my husband for safekeeping. They were kept with his manuscripts in a certain cupboard to which he had the key.

During our exile in Switzerland we came into contact with a lawyer, a Dr. Heins, whom the children knew well, and he offered to help us. My husband was delighted; he gave him the key and asked him to move the things to a safe place, which Dr. Heins did. Soon afterward the opportunity unexpectedly arose—through an acquaintance in Berlin who had a diplomat's passport, was a great bibliophile, and was allowed to travel to the United States—to get the things safely out of Germany and into Switzerland. My husband wrote to Dr. Heins, asking him to give this acquaintance of ours all the manuscripts and letters he had in his keeping, but Dr. Heins refused. He explained, "Thomas Mann is dispossessed; these things have great value, and it would be a punishable offense for me to surrender something so valuable. I can't release them." He simply refused to respect my husband's wishes, and all he did was to keep sending sizable bills for his useless efforts. Just before my husband's sixtieth birthday the confiscation was lifted for propaganda purposes. Dr. Heins sent a triumphant telegram, came to Zurich, and we celebrated. It must have been a few days after the birthday when Dr. Heins was called to the phone, returned pale and trembling, and said, "The confiscation has just been renewed." I said to him, "That was to be foreseen. It looks hopeless to me now, and I urge you to do no more about it." Then we quarreled with him because he absolutely insisted on continuing his efforts and presenting us with bills, all for nothing.

When the war was over, Klaus, who was in the American army, and Erika, who was a war correspondent, both went to Munich and immediately looked up Dr. Heins to get back the things he had been keeping. He told them his office, located in the center of the city, had been bombed; he had been able to save his own papers in the nick of time, but Thomas Mann's papers and manuscripts had all gone up in flames; he hadn't been able to get them out in time. Strange indeed. There was no way of proving whether this was true. In any case, the papers have vanished and have not been seen to this day, and all the steps we initiated proved fruitless. The official sources we turned to refused us their help, making poor excuses: Högner, the German minister of the interior at that time, and Dr. Dahn, the president of the Bar Association. Even our own lawyer seemed to be on very friendly terms with Heins, judging from the tone of his correspondence with him. We stopped our search, and I have given up all hope of ever seeing the things again.

The few letters Thomas Mann wrote me during his courtship were not destroyed, only because he asked me for them while he was writing *Royal Highness* and, orderly as he was, he didn't throw his excerpts away. Every one of them was found among his posthumous papers.

From the day we emigrated, we were almost never separated again. I accompanied him everywhere in foreign countries. In the course of all those years we were separated only twice: the first time in America, when I went to Chicago for two days, and then we telephoned each other; the second time after the war, when we were back in Switzerland and I went to Florence for the funeral of my son-in-law Borgese. Then we telephoned too. So there was no more correspondence.

To be sure, we felt quite comfortable living in Switzerland, but still, one couldn't help being nervous, and with 1938—the annexation of Austria, the Munich

Conference, the invasion of Czechoslovakia—even Switzerland's situation became questionable. It was then that we went to America. We had already been there several times, the first in 1934 on the occasion of the publication of the American edition of *The Tales of Jacob*, the first volume of *Joseph*. Blanche Knopf, the wife of our American publisher, Alfred Knopf, came to Europe every year to look for talented new authors, and when she was in Zurich, she visited us and said, "The first *Joseph* volume is to appear this summer, and my husband thought he would like to make something of a celebration out of it." Knopf's idea was to give a testimonial dinner in New York, to which Mayor La Guardia and many writers would be invited, and he wanted us to come to New York for it. Would we? Of course Alfred would cover the costs. We could discuss it and think it over. She would still be here for another two days and then we could tell her how we felt. We both agreed immediately: "There's nothing to discuss. We'd like it very much. Of course we'll come."

It was all arranged, and I then wrote a very diplomatic letter to Alfred, saying we would love to come, but the doctor had said that although Thomas Mann's health was sound, and he had no objections to his making the trip, of course he could go only if he were provided with all the comforts and conveniences. The children had requested this letter; they had advised me to write it.

We had a very pleasant crossing on a Dutch ship, the R.M.S. *Volendam*. Upon our arrival in New York, a crowd of journalists appeared with the tugboat, and

KATIA MANN

✿❖✿❖✿❖✿❖✿❖✿❖✿❖✿❖✿❖✿❖✿❖✿

there was a great to-do. We were dumfounded, and I
asked, "What's it all about?" For we didn't know that
Thomas Mann was such a well-known or famous writer
in the United States.

"Yeah, we want to see Thomas Mann of course,
you know, he's on board, Thomas Mann."

One of them asked me, "Mr. Mann of course is
Jewish?"

I said, "Not a bit."

Then there was a headline about our reception in
the newspaper: "NOT A BIT, SAYS FRAU MANN."

On the way to the hotel we had a police escort
riding in front of our car on motorcycles. Alfred Knopf
had arranged everything magnificently, and he had reserved a really lovely suite for us at the Savoy Plaza
Hotel.

I said to him, "Alfred, that's wonderful."

"I didn't forget what your doctor said," he answered slyly.

For the testimonial dinner my husband had prepared a little speech in English, and he made a terrible
faux pas toward the end of it: after he had expressed
gratitude for his warm welcome, for America's interest
in his work, and for his friend Alfred Knopf's arranging
this festive reception, he closed with the words: "He is
not only a publisher, he is a creature too." He meant to
say "creator"; I could have sunk into the ground, but
Knopf laughed.

My husband's fifty-ninth birthday also fell during
this time. He was presented with a cake with fifty-nine
candles which he was supposed to blow out in one

breath. He actually did it. That, too, was a big success.

We were there for a week and left delighted and impressed by all we had experienced.

When we went over for the second time, my husband, along with Albert Einstein, was awarded an honorary doctorate at Harvard, and we stayed with the writer Hendrik van Loon, who was very well known then. He was a popular historian who had written a world history, and was a pleasant man. While we were staying with him, we received an invitation from Roosevelt to a dinner party at the White House. We felt highly honored. It was a small group, and I can recall Roosevelt telling some tale from his student days in Munich, whereupon Mrs. Roosevelt said, "I think that was an excellent story." We all had to smile, especially after she made the same comment a second time. Later, when my husband was a guest professor at Princeton, we were invited to the White House again and stayed there for three days. When we arrived, Roosevelt was in New York State, where they had a country house, and I was very struck by Mrs. Roosevelt's naturalness and simplicity. At teatime she herself came to knock at our door: "If you would like tea now, tea is served." The White House is a very spacious building, and after all, she could have sent a servant, but no, she came herself. She was extremely nice. The next day Roosevelt returned; we had breakfast together, and the first thing he said was, "I brought some pheasant with me. Where is it? I would like it for breakfast." Well, he got it. In the evenings he mixed our cocktails himself and was very charming. As a person, he was unusually attractive, and

my husband respected him deeply. But it was such a
shame, he was in very poor health—the polio, and then
he had had a stroke. In spite of all this he was amazingly
active. He was in a wheelchair; everywhere in the
White House ramps had been put over the steps. He
couldn't walk at all, but he could swim, and there was
a swimming pool there for him. He didn't give the
impression of a sick man, for he was so lively and high-
spirited. He seemed especially taken with Erika, who
was with us.

My husband was deeply shocked by his death, and
he wrote a very moving eulogy for him. He was a much
better President than Truman, and would certainly have
had a better German policy.

In the summer of 1939 we returned to Europe one
more time. We flew to Stockholm for the P.E.N. Congress, which never took place. H. G. Wells was also
there, waiting around, and I said to him, "You must go
back to England."

"And the Congress?" he asked in astonishment.

"The Congress will not take place."

Wells wouldn't believe it.

From Malmö we flew back to London via Amsterdam. It was shortly after the outbreak of the war, a
dreadful flight. We were flying terribly low. It bothered
me, and I asked the stewardess why.

"Nazi Germany will permit us to fly over their
territory only if we fly very low. Yesterday they even
forced us to reduce our speed, and they flew so close
beside us that they could look in through all the win-
dows to find out who was in the plane."

"Oh, so that's the reason."

Then I said to my husband, "I would like to have a turn sitting next to the window."

He said, "But I always sit by the window."

"But I would like to for a change."

Well, he begrudgingly made room for me in the window seat.

Diagonally across from us sat a robust, Jewish-looking gentleman. He had obviously heard what the stewardess said, and he fainted. But nothing happened.

The next day someone on the same flight was shot to death through the window by a German air force pilot. They probably thought the man was Thomas Mann, because the Nazis of course knew about his stay in Stockholm and his return to the United States.

It was frightening in London. The English had made no preparations at all for a state of war. Whereas they had constantly been having blackout drills in Zurich—which then turned out to be unnecessary because nothing happened to neutral Switzerland—in England nothing of the sort had been done. There were no blackout curtains, and so at night you were allowed to light only a match in your bedroom, no more. The streets were filled with men and women in uniform. The mood was very strange. Then we returned on an American ship, the *Washington*, which had a triple booking. We were in first class, but the lounges had been turned into dormitories, with two cots, then a narrow passageway, and then two more cots; one dormitory for the ladies, one for the gentlemen.

We were given water by the thimbleful; there

were three sittings for each meal. A huge crowd of two thousand people was on board. Upon our arrival in New York someone from Knopf picked us up and said, "And now you are here for good."

VIII

IT WAS NOT DIFFICULT for us to establish new house-holds in America. First we were offered a house in Rhode Island for the summer by an admirer of Thomas Mann's, Miss Caroline Newton, a devotée of literature, with whom my husband had often corresponded. We were there for two months, and during that time I went to look around and found a place in Princeton. We rented it immediately. It was a very pleasant, well-furnished house, and my husband felt right at home there. It was almost as lovely as our house in Munich. Of course Princeton has changed a great deal since then. In those days it had a pleasant university, and we had a nice group of friends there. Americans by nature are very hospitable and obliging.

We had—it was still all right in those days—a Negro couple, John and Lucie. She did the cooking and cooked very well indeed, and he was the butler and also drove the car when I wasn't able to, for I was always very busy. Our servant situation was quite funny: Lucie had a brother, Horatio, whom they smuggled in. John and Horatio, both in white jackets, served the meals.

Annette Kolb was also in America then, and on a

visit to us she said, "Listen, Katia, you're doing all right!"

I said, "Well, we're elegant people, that's all. That's the way it is."

Our economic situation in Princeton was quite satisfactory. Of course I had to concern myself with the household and had my husband's whole correspondence to take care of, except for what was in English. We had to look for a secretary for the English correspondence because I couldn't write it very well. Christian Gauss, the dean of the university, helped us out. He told us that Molly Shenstone, the wife of a younger colleague, would love to work for us, but only as a volunteer; she didn't want to be paid for it. We then became good friends; I found her uncommonly sympathetic. I saw her for the last time shortly before her death in 1968—she and her husband were such lovely people.

Living nearby were the Walters, the Werfels, Max Reinhardt, Hermann Broch, and Erich von Kahler, whom my husband liked very much and respected highly. He wrote many letters to Kahler. Again there was a whole circle of emigrants gathered there, the way it had been in Sanary. Albert Einstein was also in Princeton. We were practically neighbors, and we saw him often. He was very likable but not especially stimulating. There was really something naïve and childlike in Einstein's makeup, such big innocent eyes—a dear man—but his genius was very strongly one-sided. Really an enormously specialized talent, and so he didn't strike one as impressive in everyday life. As far as his political understanding was concerned, he didn't have much to speak of. He once had a conversation with someone who came from Russia and who told him he foresaw a war between Russia and National Socialist Germany. Einstein told us about this and said, "Well, I don't know whether this is going to come about or not. But one thing I do know for sure, and that is that the Russians would be routed by the Germans and totally defeated. If I knew everything that well, then I would be a wise man." To be sure, he was by no means the only one to hold such beliefs at that time.

People will build their houses of cards. They know about the autobiographical element in Thomas Mann's writing, know that in his books he sometimes gave sketches of his friends and acquaintances, and then they begin to speculate freely. They are happy when they think they have caught him out with their detective skills. As a result, there have always been terrible misunderstandings—and there still are—not only regarding supposed models, but also in regard to alleged influences of other authors on Thomas Mann. Most striking in this connection is the hypothesis of his biographer Klaus Schröter.

In his youth my husband admired Hermann Bahr very much, for example. Bahr also influenced his style. Thomas Mann often admitted openly that as a young man he had occasionally imitated Hermann Bahr a bit. He said when you're young, you really should do something like that until you have truly found yourself. One could also point to several other early influences. More dubious, however, is that Paul Bourget influenced my husband, although Klaus Schröter has made this claim with particular emphasis. Schröter wrote the text for the illustrated monograph on Thomas Mann published by rororo:* his thesis is that, from "The Dilettante" to *Krull*, everything in fact comes from Bourget. Thomas Mann: Bourget's pupil, a clearly proven fact—according to Schröter.

This young Germanist from a good Hamburg family had just received his doctorate when he came to see me. He soon led the conversation around to Bourget. I said, "Listen, Herr Schröter, after all, I lived with the man for fifty years. I can tell you, there could hardly be another writer who spoke as much as Thomas Mann always did about what had influenced him in his life—whether it was Knut Hamsun or Dostoevsky or whoever. But I never to my recollection heard the name Bourget from him in my life."

He replied in an ironical tone that he knew all too well why that was.

Then Schröter sent me the typewritten manuscript of his text, and this time I wrote, "Dear Herr Schröter, you are really completely wrong. My husband hardly knew Bourget; he scarcely read French in his youth." Which didn't make Schröter give up his idée fixe. He simply couldn't be convinced. He claimed in addition that Bourget had exercised a very strong influence on both brothers. In Heinrich's case it would be more likely, for Heinrich was very strongly influenced by

---

* The term "rororo" refers to the paperback division of the German publishing house Rowohlt Verlag.

French literature, whereas Thomas Mann wasn't. More-over, the thesis of the direct influence of a given author on Thomas Mann must be regarded, after all, with great reservation: the psychology of decline, decadence, and aestheticism was a well-known subject of the fin de siècle. Not only Bourget and Bahr but also Nietzsche, Schopenhauer, and others treated these themes.

There is, however, a passage in *Tonio Kröger*—during the sea voyage—when Tonio recalls an essay by Bourget he had once read. The title is literally from Bourget, "about cosmological and psychological philoso-phies." Tonio thinks of this and adds, "It was quite a fine prattle." I can only ask: does an author write in such an offhand way about someone who is supposed to be so significant to him? If Bourget did indeed play a minor role in my husband's thought after all, this influence must have come to him secondhand by way of Heinrich.

The silly thing about the whole story is simply that this ridiculous Bourget legend had been introduced to the world at all. I remember that at the time a very brief review of the illustrated monograph appeared in *Der Spiegel*. All it said was: It is interesting to note the great influence which Bourget had on Thomas Mann.

And then another "discovery" of Schröter's: that Thomas Mann once contributed for a short time to a right-wing nationalistic and anti-Semitic periodical, *The Twentieth Century*. To mention this biographical detail was more than silly, it was malicious. Heinrich was twenty-four years old then, and he had been made temporary editor of the periodical in question; Thomas was twenty and was asked to write for it now and then. He came from a family of Lübeck patricians who traditionally tended to be somewhat anti-Semitic and conservative; that's the way it was in Germany. But at that time he was still an innocent in political matters.

Occasionally, then, he wrote a few pieces for *The Twentieth Century*. I think it's all right to mention this as a piquant detail. But for pages Schröter quoted from contributions to *The Twentieth Century*, and partially dishonestly at that, since he gave as Thomas Mann's own opinion what had been offered only as a paraphrase of the book he was reviewing. I wrote Schröter, "I find it entirely inappropriate, and it looks very much like a denunciation." But he wouldn't listen, and since then we have been deadly enemies.

To come back to the problem of the use of models: instead of inventing freely, Thomas Mann preferred to base himself upon reality. He liked to discover, rather than to invent, scenes, basic characteristics of people, and much else. He made what was actual his own, worked it up in his own fashion, animated it, as he said, with his artistry. Like quite a few other great figures in the history of literature, he sometimes gave his models occasion for annoyance because they naïvely identified themselves with the poetic product. The scale of possible reactions extends, let us say, from the response of the Wunderkind's widow to the case of Annette Kolb.

The Wunderkind really existed; he was a little Greek pianist, dressed up in the outfit my husband gives him in the novella, white satin from head to foot; and he died very young. Years later his widow wrote to

Erika that he had known the story and been very amused by it, and she enclosed a photograph of the Wunderkind attired as he is in the novella. Here, then, there was no offense taken. Nor had any been intended.

But what happened with Annette Kolb was really regrettable. Annette Kolb is the physical model for a character in *Dr. Faustus,* Jeanette Scheurl—even the name betrays a similarity to Annette. But it is said of this figure, who really is portrayed with love and respect, that she had "an elegant sheep's face." This offended Annette so greatly that from then on it was all over between her and Thomas Mann. He always had an especially high opinion of Annette Kolb. As mentioned earlier, I had known her when I was a child. She was considerably older than I and was always out of the ordinary in a humorous way. She never, as a matter of fact, laid any claim to feminine beauty, and was brought up by her very pretty sister Germaine with the idea that she was thin and scrawny; on this point Annette said, "So what, a salt shaker is better than an overstuffed quilt." She used to say that back in the days when she was a guest in my parents' house. She always spoke a distinctly Bavarian dialect, which was the custom in Munich—even the aristocracy spoke dialect, and although the Kolbs were no aristocrats, they did have a salon and gave afternoon receptions à la Parisienne attended by court society and all sorts of people.

Annette's mother was French. Her brother was an officer in the Royal Regiment, which was usually reserved for the nobility. Her father was the director of the Botanical Gardens in Munich, and they had a very pretty, old-fashioned little house that went with the post. At some point the rumor arose that Annette was a Wittelsbach, but I don't think so; I would never believe that of her mother. Theirs was a delightful household, half French, with its connections with the court circles; and they all spoke either French or Bavarian dialect.

As a writer Annette had her own peculiar, special talent. She didn't know German very well; I mean, of course she knew German, but she couldn't write it. I can remember a sentence in one of her works: "It seemed to him that the furnace wasn't playing anymore."

Moreover, in certain matters she was very naïve. After I was married and had had one or two children, I went to a performance of *Faust* with her, and during the scene with Gretchen at the well (when the audience learns of Gretchen's pregnancy), she nudged me and asked, "Tell me, Katia, has the tragedy already happened?" That was her idea of a "tragedy." That's the way she was.

She was very funny. There couldn't be anyone less out to please men; and it wouldn't have suited her either, yet she always made a deep secret of her age. We figured out that she must have been a hundred and three when she died. This was based on a specific fact. Annette had written her memoirs when she was in America. In 1933 she emigrated voluntarily because of her convictions, as did René Schickele, her best friend. First, she went to Paris, and then she went to America, where she was terribly unhappy, didn't fit in at all, and besides that, was ill much of the time. I often went to see her in her hotel in New York, and she was very grateful when anyone showed concern about her. She had gone to America because she thought she would be secure there, safer from the Nazis, which admittedly was the case. But she simply didn't like it over there, and in 1945, just as soon as possible, she returned to Paris.

Bermann Fischer and Fritz Landshoff had jointly founded a New York publishing house, the L. B. Fischer Corporation, which was not very successful because they weren't familiar with local business conditions. Now, Annette had given her memoirs to Landshoff for publication; he read them and then returned them to her. Annette told me that Landshoff had said he found it all very interesting, and that the scene in which she fled from Paris with her parents in 1870 was especially vivid and good. Suddenly she seemed confused. She said, "Yes, yes, of course; but wait a minute, that's perfect nonsense. That will have to come out. I wasn't even alive then!" The fact was that the episode, in which she must have been at least two or three years old, revealed that she had been born not much later than 1865. That was why the episode had to be eliminated.

After my husband's death we still went on seeing each other as friends. When she visited me several years ago, not long before her death, she told me, among other things, "You know, Katia, I just got a new passport."

I: "Oh? That's good. Had your old one expired?"

"Yes, and you know, the man asked me my age,

and I said to him, 'It's *my* age after all, isn't it? It's not yours, and it's none of your business, is it? You have your age and I have mine.' And he said, 'All right, put down whatever you like for me.' " That was the last time I saw her—a most unusual personality.

IX

T HE GUEST PROFESSORSHIP at Princeton didn't last
forever. It was extended for another year, but
then it ended in 1940. The summer of 1940 we spent in
California, and we were highly enthusiastic about that
part of the country and its climate. The California land-
scape reminded us very much of Israel. My husband
liked it, and we soon found a beautiful, relatively inexpensive piece of property which we proceeded to buy.
Some Hollywood film man had purchased it but had
lost interest, and then had let it go for a bargain price.
The location was beautiful, with a magnificent view of
the sea and of Catalina Island, and with palm, orange,
and lemon trees on a large plot. Then we found a very
good architect, and our interior decorator was the son
of the formerly very wealthy Berlin coal magnate
Huldschinsky. This extraordinarily cultivated émigré
eked out a living as a decorator, and he came to me
and asked whether he might not do our house for us. I
said, "Dear Paul, I have every confidence in you, but
we simply can't afford it, you know."

To which he replied, "I would charge practically
nothing, just enough to cover expenses; but if it gets

around in Hollywood that I decorated Thomas Mann's house—that would really help me, it would give me a good name."

"But then of course you must do it."

And he did a beautiful job. It was a charming house. My husband always said it was the best study he ever had, and he felt completely at home there. The climate is especially pleasant because it never gets too hot, except, strangely enough, in October. Then the wind from the desert sometimes blew so hot and so dry that the paper in the typewriter curled right up. It was oppressive.

The nights were always cool, and one really couldn't have asked for anything better. The beach was only ten to twelve minutes away by car. Every day I drove my husband to the promenade overlooking the ocean, and while he took a walk, I went swimming. I drove him there and picked him up again. I never accompanied him on his walks, except perhaps a little way now and then. He liked to walk alone, and I am sure that on these walks he was always already thinking out and arranging in his mind what he was going to write the next day. This was a time when he was completely undisturbed, and I don't think it would have been right for me to go along. But every couple of days a car would stop and someone would ask, "May we give you a ride?" Then he would say, "No, thank you, I'd rather walk," and usually all the dogs would follow him. Americans don't walk much; in any case, they didn't at that time.

Now we had built the house in Pacific Palisades,

with a mortgage of course, for we were never "rich." My husband went on many lecture tours—we needed the money; we had to have something. In the beginning Erika accompanied us because of the "question periods." In those days Thomas Mann couldn't yet give very fluent answers in English, but Erika could, so he would tell her how she should answer a given question for him. Then she would say, "My father says . . . ," proceeding to give a very free translation.

I can still remember that we were once at a college in the vicinity of Long Island, and Erika wasn't with us. "What are we going to do about the question period?" I asked. There was a teacher there, an émigrée. "I speak English and German," she told us, "and since your daughter isn't here, I would be very glad to do it for you."

"Good, we're very grateful," I said.

So the question period came, and she handled it like this: "Mr. Mann says, and I sink he is quite right in dis . . ." No one had asked for her opinion, and it was quite painful to have to listen to her, especially in her inadequate English. I don't know whether Tommy liked these question periods. It was an American custom, and he got used to them.

In January 1944 we became American citizens. The citizenship tests were not easy by any means. You had to study quite hard; not only did you have to be reasonably informed about the Constitution and the branches of government, but you also had to know something about the government and legislature of the individual states and cities, which was much more difficult. All in all, it was rather tricky, as I recall, but we both passed. I had studied more than my husband, but he was clever and skillful enough to gloss over the points that weren't quite clear to him and to talk his way around the lady who was examining him. He wrote her a nice dedication in her copy of *Buddenbrooks*. She handed it to the judge, and then the judge wanted to have one too. Thus, the affair turned out very agreeably.

Max Horkheimer and his wife were witnesses, and afterward when we celebrated the successful outcome together in a restaurant, Horkheimer told us that when asked under oath whether Thomas Mann would be a desirable citizen, he had answered, "You bet!"

The whole matter was somewhat distressing to my husband because of his Czechoslovakian citizenship, which had been granted to him in 1936 when his German citizenship was revoked. He wrote a long letter to Czech President Eduard Beneš, whom he admired, explaining to him that he hoped Beneš wouldn't regard the change as ingratitude, but that since we were now living in this country and would continue to live here, and since the time for taking out our American citizenship was almost up, we had had to take this step. Beneš sent him a nice answer.

A whole colony of German refugees—literary people, musicians, film and theater people—had settled in California; most of them had arrived after us and were able to get there only with our help. Where there are good neighbors, good friends, a stimulating circle—there is life and a feeling of being at home. Among the musicians were Schönberg, Eisler, and Walter, and there must have been two dozen writers or more. In the world of émigrés everyone has open house, and so in California we saw more German writers than we had in Munich. We were friendly with the Franks, and especially with the Werfels, whom we saw a good deal of. I liked Franz Werfel in particular. He was very gifted artistically, tremendously musical, and so outgoing and amiable. Unlike most of the émigrés, Werfel made a very good living in America. His *Song of Bernadette* was an immediate success. It became a Book-of-the-Month Club selection and then a movie—he made a great deal of money, unlike us in our first years. We made our first large sum when the Book-of-the-Month Club selected *Joseph in Egypt*. By then Franz Werfel was ill; he was suffering from a serious heart condition. When I went to their house, he was in bed. I said to him, "Just imagine, now *Joseph* has become a Book-of-the-Month Club selection." He was so happy that he turned red with pleasure. "Alma! Alma!" he called, "come here; you must hear this. Isn't that splendid?" He was always embarrassed because he earned so much more than the rest of the émigrés, and when my husband had this success, his first great success after coming to America, Werfel was really as happy as a child about it. He was a lovable person indeed.

Alma Mahler-Werfel was of course a personality in her own right. My husband thought a great deal of her. She always drank far too many sweet liqueurs and was rather malicious by nature. She loved to start gossip, and it was she who got Arnold Schönberg going on the business of the twelve-tone system in *Faustus*, telling him that Thomas Mann had stolen his theory of atonal composition. Thomas Mann was friendly with Schönberg, and borrowed the composer's *Theory of Harmony* to study, but there can be no question of theft. Schönberg hadn't even read *Dr. Faustus* yet; he could only have had that from Alma. He held the whole thing very much against my husband, and therefore the second printing of the book carried an author's note to the effect that Schönberg and not Adrian Leverkühn was the originator of this theory of composition. This mollified Schönberg.

Alma was rather mean, but she did radiate a certain aura; she had a strong personality. She was difficult to get along with, and she gave her former husband Gustav Mahler a very difficult time. She alienated him from all his friends and made him break off with his female admirers. Mahler died young. I think she was rather too much for his nervous system.

Schönberg was not a very winning man, and I took an immediate dislike to his wife, Gertrud, but she didn't have a very easy time of it with her tyrannical husband. We were neighbors, and they sometimes invited us over. The guests were tyrannized in that Schönberg couldn't stand cigarette smoke, and his wife had to forbid their guests to smoke, which was really very unpleasant for people like my daughter Erika, a passionate smoker; if she couldn't have a cigarette after dinner, it made her feel ill.

The Schönbergs had two boys who were so terribly ill-behaved that there was always the chance that they would come downstairs in their nightshirts when their parents had guests for dinner and say, "We want to have something too." The only way of keeping them quiet at all was to let them sleep in their parents' beds and to have their pretty older sister Nuria (who later married a musician named Nono) keep an eye on them. Otherwise parents and guests would have had no peace at dinner.

At the Schönbergs' everything was a bit topsy-turvy. Gertrud Schönberg was hardly less difficult than her husband, about whom—as I heard at the time—she was very concerned. He was no longer young, he wasn't in good health, and he didn't have the slightest success in America. One of his ill-behaved boys later became the best tennis player at his college and won many prizes, which naturally made Schönberg very proud. But one day he and his wife went for a walk, and on the way a young couple came toward them. The young woman whispered something to her husband, and they both looked at Schönberg very closely as they went by. Schönberg stopped and turned around to look at the young couple, who had also stopped and turned around. He was just able to catch the young wife saying to her husband, "That was Schönberg's father."

Schönberg had a heart condition, and he was very superstitious. He was afraid of the number 13 and firmly believed that he would someday die on the thirteenth of the month. After all, he was already seventy-six. When the thirteenth arrived, he was always restless; in the evening Gertrud Schönberg would have

to sit with him and hold his hand. On the other side of
the room was a clock, and he would watch it until the
thirteenth was past. On July 13, 1951, exactly the same
thing happened. They were sitting there, and the clock
was ticking; finally midnight came. Schönberg went
upstairs to go to bed. Gertrud Schönberg went as always to the kitchen to fix his bedtime drink—he always
drank a cup of Bovril at night. When she took the cup
up to him, he was lying dead in his room. Gertrud was
terrified and looked at the clock. She had become just
as obsessed with the clock as he. She saw that it wasn't
yet midnight; the clock in the room downstairs had
been several minutes fast. Someone told me that from
that time on Gertrud Schönberg tormented herself with
the idea that perhaps he had only been frightened by the
clock and that he might not have died if the upstairs
clock hadn't indicated that midnight was not yet past.

I couldn't even say where we met Hanns Eisler. I
scarcely believe it was at the Schönbergs'. In any case,
we saw him frequently; he was often at our house and
we at his. My husband always found him very entertain-
ing, especially his critical remarks about Wagner. He
always said, "Just listen—that passage, for example, it's
—all I can say is, that old rascal!"

Because of their extraordinarily divergent views,
they had very lively conversations. Eisler was always
ready to contradict, and he saw through Wagner's ef-
fects so well. They also talked about Hans Pfitzner,
about his *Palestrina*, a work which my husband liked
and which he even felt to be kindred to him in spirit.
Eisler came right out and called it one of the oldest of

chestnuts. My husband liked to listen to him. He was really very well educated, full of esprit and actually very amusing.

Charlie Chaplin was someone we also saw frequently. We saw him at Viertel's and also at Eisler's. Eisler liked Chaplin very much, and so did my husband, who was the most appreciative audience imaginable— he was never happier at a party than when someone was telling stories. He didn't care much for profound intellectual conversation. He could listen to Chaplin for hours on end, and Chaplin told fascinating stories about his youth, his first theatrical experiences, and his failures —all this in a very comical, lively, droll manner. He didn't act out his anecdotes: he was simply a very amusing storyteller. My husband loved this and sat there laughing until he cried; he kept having to wipe his eyes and was obviously delighted to the nth degree. Later I visited Chaplin again in Vevey, where he had a beautiful estate, but by that time my husband was no longer alive.

Between Bert Brecht and my husband there was no love lost. Somehow or other they just didn't click. We saw him occasionally in California; in Germany my husband hadn't met him at all. In Munich, Therese Giehse once brought Thomas Mann a play by Brecht. Therese was a friend of both my husband and Brecht, and when my husband returned the play to her after he had read it, he said, "Just imagine, the monster has talent." Therese passed this backhanded compliment on to Brecht. He responded testily, although flattered,

"As a matter of fact, I always found his short stories quite good." Other than that, Thomas Mann knew very little of Brecht; I believe their hostility was mutual. As far as I know, Brecht never read a Mann novel.

In connection with *Mother Courage*, someone once asked me, "Do you know why there is a dumb girl in this play?" "No, I don't," I replied. For it is surely rather surprising to have a dumb girl in a play. The response was: "Brecht created the role for his wife because when he wrote the play, they hadn't been in Sweden long enough to learn the language. Helene Weigel didn't know Swedish, and so he created the role of a dumb girl for her." In any case, that's the way it was told to me.

Brecht's speech in his own defense before the Committee on Un-American Activities was broadcast on the radio, and I heard it. Brecht was very sly indeed: he pretended to be stupid, and the others *were* stupid. This whole business of loyalty checks was a great disaster, and today it's almost as bad again. We experienced the whole so-called McCarthy era; during it my husband was continually attacked as a Communist, which he never was in his life.

Alfred Döblin had also emigrated to America, but had not been able to establish himself because he had no public there and hence no success; this made him very bitter. He always had angry words to say about

Thomas Mann, whose reputation and success in America were constantly growing, in contrast to his own. There are some people who have the feeling that there is only a certain amount of success in the world, and that another's diminishes their own. Unfortunately, Döblin shared this feeling to some degree. Americans didn't take to his things, but of course my husband couldn't help that; he took every opportunity to bring Döblin to people's attention and to see that he received financial support. For the celebration of Döblin's sixty-fifth birthday, a collection was even taken, and of course we contributed to it.

Things went very badly for Döblin, for the emergency contracts at M-G-M and Warner Brothers expired after a year. These pro forma contracts had made it possible for a whole series of refugee writers, among them Heinrich Mann, to emigrate to America as "scriptwriters" and at least initially to have a guaranteed livelihood, even though they were paid practically nothing for their services. My husband used his influence to try to get an extension of contract for several authors, including Döblin. But Döblin rewarded his efforts only by losing his temper whenever my husband's name came up. In 1945, when he returned to the French-occupied zone of Germany right after the war, his hatred came into the open. Döblin was given the rank of a French colonel and edited a German periodical called *The Golden Gate* on behalf of the French government. In it he published hateful articles against Thomas Mann by a man named Lüth. About *The Magic Mountain*, which

Lüth apparently hadn't even read (in any case he didn't know it well), he wrote, "and an especially unsuccessful figure is that of the ascetic woman Naphta."

In general, this Lüth invented all kinds of curious, false, and stupid things about the book. Paul Rilla then wrote a reply to this really unusually foolish essay, with its lady by the name of Naphta. It was disgraceful to what degree and by what means Döblin sought to persecute and denigrate Thomas Mann. He didn't have to do that. His own literary accomplishments were, after all, considerable enough, as were his own creative powers.

Paul Rilla has now been dead for a long time. When my husband read his reply, he thanked him profusely. Walter Rilla, Paul's brother, is still alive; he is a well-regarded writer and also a very good actor. In the film of *Felix Krull* he played the role of Lord Kilmarnock. We still write to each other from time to time.

Heinrich Mann was very unhappy in America. He and his wife had also received an entrance visa based on a pro forma contract with the Hollywood studios, but Heinrich was completely unknown in America. With the exception of *Henri Quatre*, nothing of his had been translated, and apart from a few émigrés, no one knew anything about him. The first volume of *Henri Quatre*, published by L.B.F., was a definite success, the second one much less so, and thus he continued to be ignored. That was unjust, and truly sad; my husband suffered because of it. Heinrich lived in poverty and in an eccentric sort of seclusion; we helped him out as much as we could. He initially received financial support from Maksim Litvinov, the Soviet ambassador to the United States, but that wasn't sufficient, and finally it stopped coming. Litvinov passed along to Heinrich the royalties from the sale of his books in Russia, but this was not enough to live on, so we were always stepping in.

The story that after his lung operation Thomas Mann received ampules and other medications from Litvinov is pure myth. Nothing of the sort happened, nor was it necessary, because my husband recovered amazingly well from the operation. He was just seventy at the time, and they said in the hospital that it was the first time they had performed such a serious lung operation on a man of his age. They did the same operation on a man of thirty-five, but my husband regained his strength more quickly than this much younger patient. Thomas Mann believed that he would die at seventy like his mother; he even wrote about it and was also interviewed on the subject, but I can't imagine that he actually believed it. He wasn't really superstitious. He was devoted to the number 7, and he was devoted to his mother too, but I doubt that he was seriously convinced that he would in fact die at the age of seventy. He said then that this dangerous illness had been an ersatz death and, further, that he might not have recovered so quickly if he hadn't been so eager to return to work as soon as possible. At the time, he was writing *Dr. Faustus*, and above all else he wanted to finish the book.

When the illness was diagnosed, I was in a very difficult situation. No one was there: the children were away at war, and the entire responsibility was mine. I was surrounded on all sides by people advising me to call in this and that doctor, telling me I should do this, that, and the other. I called in a specialist, a Dr. Rosenthal. He examined my husband, and when I asked him, "Well, what do you think?" he answered, "It's a malignant growth, cancer—and now we are going upstairs to tell the patient to be patient." I said, "We are not going upstairs and we are not going to tell him."

Later I explained to Tommy, "Dr. Rosenthal gave you a thorough examination, and apparently you do have an abscess on the lung, which really ought to be removed, and we should get to a first-rate lung surgeon as soon as possible." I made inquiries; I called up Martin Gumpert, who, in addition to being the model for Mai-Sachme in the last volume of *Joseph*, was also a very good doctor, and a Dr. Adams in Chicago was recommended as absolutely first rate. In no time at all we got my husband to Chicago, but then it took quite a while before the preliminary examinations were evaluated. They also did a bronchoscopy, which confirmed the growth. The operation which followed was completely successful. Basically, my husband knew exactly what was involved, but he didn't want to be told. When Heinrich heard that Tommy had to have an operation, he was beside himself and very concerned. He told me he wanted to go with us to Chicago. I dissuaded him—with difficulty—because I knew that it would upset my husband tremendously. Heinrich's intentions were good, but I could only tell him, "Heinrich, please don't do it. Tommy would think that this was the end. Please, you mustn't." Then he sent him a telegram to the hospital; I didn't even show it to my husband because it expressed such deep concern that my husband could only have thought his life was in grave danger. Thank God, that wasn't the case.

Surprisingly, Heinrich became more and more attached to his younger brother. His devotion grew with the years, along with his modesty. He wasn't joking when he once told me in the course of a conversation, "Of the two of us, Tommy is greater; that is certain, and I am quite aware of it." He was sincere about this and had the deepest respect for his brother. He once said to Erika, "Your father and I now see eye to eye on political matters, only your father is somewhat more radical."

After Heinrich lost his wife, he lived with us for a while until I found him a new place, and then, helpless as he was, I more or less looked after him throughout the following years. Nelly's case was not a pleasant one. While she was still alive, we were constantly receiving telephone calls that she had been found in a ditch again. She had learned to drive in California, and she often drove when she was drunk. Drunken driving is a serious offense. Twice she was taken to a sanitarium, and she frequently attempted suicide. Finally, on the fifth try, she took her own life with an overdose of sleeping tablets.

Heinrich suffered very much from her depressions and then from her death. The loss of his wife made him more isolated than ever. He called us up one day, and when I asked, "Well, Heinrich, how are things with you two?" he said, "Not good. Nelly just died." That's the way he was—very strange.

He was also very proud. He and Nelly had an

old-fashioned apartment which in my opinion was uncomfortable and not very attractive. It was located close
to Los Angeles, quite a distance from us. Whenever
Heinrich visited us, I always picked him up in our car
and then took him home again. After Nelly died, his
landlord told him he had to move. For a while rents had
been frozen, but then the rent controls were removed
again. Heinrich was very attached to the apartment because it was filled with memories of Nelly, and he
absolutely didn't want to leave. He composed a letter
that had to be translated into English, and it included
the statement, "Mr. Mann will not give up this apartment because he doesn't want to and he doesn't have
to."

But he did have to. I found him a very pleasant
place in Santa Monica, not far from us, which was
naturally much better for me, as well as for him. It
really was exactly what he needed. The house had a
lovely big living room with an alcove for dining, a
kitchen, bath, and two bedrooms—one for him and one
for his housekeeper, who was also a trained nurse, an
émigrée with whom he was better off than with any of
his strange wives. She took excellent care of him.

I thought it a fortunate arrangement, and I said,
"Heinrich, I've found something really nice for you. I
think you'll like it. Let's drive over there this afternoon
and take a look at it." Well, I showed it all to him: "Just
look at this lovely large living room, and there is room
for your shelves—you can put your bookcases there.
And there is your bedroom and that one is for the help."
He responded, "Yes, and where does one dine?"

I said, "Heavens, Heinrich, I thought over there in the corner of the living room. How about putting the round table and the dining room chairs there? I mean, you ordinarily don't give large dinner parties. And the kitchen is over there, with an opening to pass food through." Where does one dine, indeed! He had his pretensions and expressed them with this peculiar mixture of formality and humor. Finally, he accepted the place graciously; I fixed everything up for him, and he moved in.

The older he became, the more attached he was to Lübeck; he even read *Buddenbrooks* again, and in his old age he spoke with a Lübeck accent that became stronger and stronger. One day some old acquaintance from Lübeck, a lawyer with whom Heinrich hadn't even been on friendly terms, wrote him a letter. This acquaintance liked to paint, and he asked Heinrich to send him some oil paints. Heinrich called me immediately: "Katia, this gentleman urgently needs some oils. Would you please get them right away and send them to him?" I said, "Heinrich, this is the week before Christmas. I have a tremendous lot to do now. All the children are coming, and I have so much to buy and so many things to take care of. Can't we wait and do it right after the holidays?"

He: "Look, Katia, you're much too conscientious not to do it. Why not right away then?"

So I did it "right away."

He still lived to receive the appointment as president of the Academy of Letters in East Berlin. It was wonderful, but at the same time I regarded it with grave concern because Heinrich was in poor health, and I thought that they would make a great show of him; he would have to give speeches and be exhausted by public appearances which he was no longer up to. I wrote to the academy to say that when he came, he would have to be treated with great consideration: he was not somebody who could stand up at a meeting and talk; great solicitude and care must be taken. He didn't live to experience it, and perhaps it was better that way, although a few last years of recognition and honors would have been more than desirable after a decade in an America that took no notice of him.

He had a very easy death. One morning his nurse called me up. "Herr Mann won't wake up. His heart is still beating, but he's lying there unconscious—he won't wake up." I told her, "That doesn't sound good at all. You had better send for a doctor." The doctor's immediate diagnosis was a cerebral hemorrhage. Heinrich had spent his last evening by the radio listening to music. He loved Italian music, and a local station had broadcast a Puccini concert that evening—Puccini, of whom Heinrich had been so especially fond. He had listened to the music and then, happy and in good spirits, he had gone to bed and fallen asleep, never to wake up again. He was seventy-eight, and his death occurred shortly before his birthday on March 27. Golo's birthday falls on the same day, and Heinrich had said to his nephew, "We'll have to have a celebration on March twenty-seventh, won't we? Be sure to come over!" Golo was then a professor at Claremont, a college a few hours away by car. But

Heinrich insisted, "You must come, Golo—see to it that you can get away." It never took place.

The Adornos also lived in California, and Adorno, Wiesengrund-Adorno, advised Thomas Mann on musical matters for *Dr. Faustus.* My husband got along with him very well, and in *The Story of a Novel* he expressed his gratitude for Adorno's advice and for his helpful support. Bruno Walter didn't advise him. Nor did Schönberg—although my husband did draw him out in conversation about many matters when he visited us or we him, and I think Schönberg enjoyed it too. My husband read portions of his novel to Bruno Walter, who took offense at the thought expressed in it that music could signify something so sinister, so demoniacally dangerous, an out-and-out pact with the devil. He didn't want to hear of such a thing. Why music? For how can music, something as sublime as music, which suffers the little children to come unto it, endanger someone so? He wasn't prepared to acknowledge that at all.

My husband's actual adviser was Wiesengrund-Adorno. His advice was of a technical nature, and he was a genuine expert. I think there was little argument between them; everything went smoothly, and my husband probably didn't contradict him. They talked together, my husband asked him questions, but Adorno never dictated anything.

Since Adrian Leverkühn was a modern composer, there is no doubt that Adorno was able to advise my husband on his hero's late compositions, such as the *Apocalypsis cum figuris,* as well as on Kretschmar's in-

terpretations of Beethoven's Piano Sonata Opus 111;
nevertheless, these passages are entirely in my husband's
own words. Adorno called his attention to many points,
explained them to him, and gave him the technical
terminology.

It's a big mistake for Adorno to think in retrospect
that he was the actual author of the book, merely because music does play a major role in it. At times he
acted positively foolishly with his pretentiousness and
conceit. It was quite funny, and there are several curious
anecdotes about "his" *Faustus.* We had a mutual friend,
Eva Herrmann, who did excellent caricatures and had
very good taste. Eva had built a charming house, but it
was small, and she could never invite more than a few
friends at a time for dinner. She had a large living room,
but there was room for only six people at table, and so
she always invited another six or eight for coffee and
schnapps after dinner. The Adornos had been there for
dinner two weeks earlier, and now it was our turn,
along with another couple. On this occasion a little
mishap occurred, a short circuit in the electric stove,
and dinner was delayed for about forty minutes. Thus
the after-dinner guests came too early, at around quarter
past nine, and the first to arrive were the Adornos. Our
hostess ran right out into the living room and said,
"There's been a little mishap. Our dinner was delayed
for forty minutes, and I'm terribly sorry, but we'll still
be at the table for a little while. If you want to take a
look at the new magazines in the meantime, the latest
New Yorker is there; perhaps that will interest you. Just
make yourselves at home." To this Wisengrund-Adorno

responded, "That you should make me wait here like this is such an affront to Thomas Mann that I really can't accept it. It's incomprehensible."

It was a peculiar attitude, this self-identification with Thomas Mann. One afternoon my husband had lain down to rest after lunch, as he always did, and I was busy with something or other. The room where I was sitting had a door leading to the garden; the door was open, and suddenly I saw Wiesengrund-Adorno coming through the yard wearing a dark suit. He came in, and I said, "Herr Doktor, all dressed up and coming through the yard?" But he looked very serious and formal. "Yes, it's a very unpleasant matter," and then he asked if he could speak with my husband. I answered, "No, you know that he's sleeping, but if you will wait for half an hour . . ." So he sat down with me, and while we were talking he suddenly began to speak of his grave concern: my husband hadn't mentioned Horkheimer in *The Story of a Novel*. I said, "What do you mean? Herr Horkheimer is a dear friend, but he doesn't have anything at all to do with *The Story of a Novel* or with *Dr. Faustus*. The fact that *you* helped my husband has surely been fully documented." But Wiesengrund-Adorno said, "No, no, it's impossible. Horkheimer is going to be deeply offended."

I: "Well, what shall we do then?"

He: "I see only one possibility—that your husband at least review Horkheimer's new book now, perhaps in *The New York Times*."

And that's the way the matter was handled. The book turned out to be by Horkheimer and Adorno: it was their *Dialectic of Enlightenment*. My husband received a copy, and he said to Golo, "I don't understand anything about this. Couldn't you write the review?" Golo wrote it, and it was published in *The New York Times* under his father's name.

One day—it must have been in 1952 or 1953, when we were already back in Europe and living in Switzerland again—some students from Frankfurt visited us from the Sociological Institute, where Adorno taught. They held a kind of interview with my husband and asked him about Adorno. My husband said, "Yes, yes, Adorno was very helpful to me on musical matters." Then I added, "True, but that's no reason for Adorno to believe he wrote the book." The students reported this to Adorno, and naturally it did not endear me to him very much. But after all, facts still do take precedence over vanity, don't they?

Thomas Mann's method of writing was unusual. When he was working on a book, he immersed himself to an extraordinary degree in the relevant subject matter, learning all he could right up until the book was finished. He got hold of everything worth knowing on the topic, collecting a mass of material, but as soon as the book was finished, he forgot it all again. He was no longer interested in it.

For *Dr. Faustus* he was, among other things, a great musical theorist; for *Joseph*, a great Egyptologist, Orientalist, and scholar of the history of religions; he

was a student of medicine for *The Magic Mountain*—
but he forgot all the resources he had used to acquire
this knowledge, as well as the knowledge itself, with
remarkable haste.

That's the way it was with everything. He didn't
have the characteristics of a scholar. He took only what
he needed and didn't want more. He once said as a
joke that he didn't know any more about a subject than
appeared in his work, so he shouldn't be quizzed or
examined beyond that.

But, as I have already said, he was always interested in music. That was the exception, for he never
lost this predilection. On the other hand, my son
Michael all of a sudden had enough of music. To be
sure, there is a difference between an amateur's interest
and a professional career, but while we were still in
America Michael suddenly said that he was tired of
music, of always playing pieces which people didn't
even want to hear. Besides, giving concerts and the
whole business connected with it made him nervous; he
just didn't like it anymore. He had studied the violin,
but on the advice of his teacher over there, the notable
violinist Henri Temianka, he switched to the viola.
Temianka had told him, "You know, your prospects
will be better if you switch from violin to viola, since
there are so many outstanding violinists and so few
violists." And then Michael was engaged right off as
violist with the San Francisco Symphony Orchestra
and spent several years there. Later he made a name for
himself as a viola soloist, giving many concerts and

going on extended tours. Now, the classical literature for viola is not very large, and so he specialized in modern music, which I have always found ugly, and he could play all the pieces from memory. I never understood how he could do it. He was very musical and highly regarded, but suddenly he gave it all up and, approaching forty, went to Harvard to begin graduate study. And strangely enough, he didn't take his Ph.D. in musicology but in Germanic languages and literatures. He then received an appointment as assistant professor at Berkeley, where he is now full professor.

It is his great good fortune to have the wife he has, my very dear and delightful daughter-in-law Gret. She's an excellent homemaker. She was a school friend of Elisabeth's, and way back then they took long trips together. Medi had an ancient little Fiat that we called "the Miracle," because it was a miracle that it still ran, and in "the Miracle" they drove to Italy and all over the place. Soon Gret and Michael got engaged, and after we went to America, Gret joined us, and then they got married. Michael was so ridiculously young when he got married that the sacristan asked, "Now, where is the bridegroom?" Michael answered, "That's me!"

"That's you?" He just couldn't believe it. Michael was nineteen or twenty and looked even younger.

Now they have celebrated their silver wedding anniversary and they have two sons; one of them, Frido, as a little boy was the model for Nepomuk Schneidewein in *Faustus*. My husband loved this grandson dearly. When he wrote to Bruno Walter about his plan to give little Fridolin a role in the novel, Walter expressed great pleasure, saying that it was a wonderful idea and he could imagine this chapter as an allegretto moderato. He had no way of knowing that in the book the child Echo would necessarily have to come to an entirely different sort of end.

X

WE STAYED IN CALIFORNIA until 1952, but America had changed so much after Roosevelt's death, especially during the so-called McCarthy era, that we no longer felt at home there. We intended to wait and see what direction political developments would take, and we certainly had no definite plans to move yet. In any case, we didn't feel drawn back to Germany; there was still too much hatred and misunderstanding there. That left Switzerland, which we had always enjoyed. But in spite of this attachment, we still might have remained in America if things had gone differently and Stevenson had become president, for example. As it was, we went to Europe every year, first by boat and then finally by plane, which was most impractical and expensive. I said, "It would make more sense to stay in Switzerland and fly to America occasionally."

In 1949, the bicentennial of Goethe's birth, we found ourselves in Germany for the first time in sixteen years. First we were in Frankfurt, where my husband gave his Goethe address in St. Paul's Church, and after that we went on to Weimar. That was our stipulation: to visit both Goethe cities, Frankfurt and Weimar, and my husband referred to our plan specifically in his speech in Frankfurt: "For me there is only one Germany, a Germany that is whole and not divided into zones, and as you know, I will go from here to Weimar." When he said that, I heard the people around me whispering and asking, "Does that mean he's a Communist?" Many people held this trip to Weimar against him. In addition, the consulate in Frankfurt pointed out that of course it didn't have the right to prevent an American citizen from traveling to Weimar, but they just wanted to call the fact to our attention that it would be viewed with great disfavor. We said, "Well, that's the way you'll have to view it. What does it matter?" After this first stay in Germany, we felt little desire to return, but we did go back a few times when we received special invitations.

In 1954, more than twenty years after our emigration, we returned to the Rhineland for the first time. My husband was scheduled to give a lecture at the university in Cologne; he read from *Felix Krull,* and then in the fall of the same year *Confessions of Felix Krull, Confidence Man* appeared. The Cologne Germanist Wilhelm Emrich had arranged for the reading; he also wrote my husband that he thought Ernst Bertram, who was living in Marienburg near Cologne, would like to use this occasion to resume contact and would welcome a reconciliation between the two of them. My husband answered, well, all right, he had nothing against it.

In the beginning we hadn't wanted to see Bertram. After Germany's defeat things went very badly for him. The Americans didn't want to de-Nazify him; he lost

his position and therefore was to receive no pension.
Then Bertram's friends approached my husband with
the plea that he take up Bertram's cause. This my husband did. He wrote a letter to the authorities in question, saying that he, Thomas Mann, had heard such and
such about Bertram's plight, that one ought to bear in
mind that he was a very noted scholar and a creative
artist, but that for a time he had made some grave
errors resulting from his concept of Germanism. His
beliefs were mistaken, to be sure; he had been a so-called
Edelnazi but he hadn't done anything really bad. Bertram got his pension and was permitted to publish once
again.

Bertram attended the lecture in Cologne, but we
didn't see him there. When we visited him at his house
in Cologne-Marienburg, as had been arranged, we dis-
covered that he was already very hard of hearing and
hadn't understood a word of the lecture. He was terribly excited and cordial and was apparently most happy
to see us. There was something decidedly old-maidish
about him. The rooms were filled with memorabilia of
his various godchildren and knickknacks and things like
that. We looked it all over, and then we were about
to leave. Suddenly he said, "Actually I had prepared
some refreshments." His excitement over our visit was
so great that he had almost forgotten the usual amenities. "How charming," we said; whereupon he brought
out all manner of delicacies, and we stayed and ate with
him. While we were there, he said, "Well, naturally,
living in Germany, one had no possible way of gaining
perspective and seeing the way things really were; one

didn't even know about most of what was happening. . . ." And I said, "Yes, of course, one couldn't gain perspective, I understand that completely. You couldn't be expected to; we could see it only from a distance."

It went very well, and we parted on friendly terms. But then later I became quite annoyed with him. Tommy had sent him one of the first copies of *Krull*, with a nice inscription: "Cordially dedicated to my old-new friend Ernst Bertram." And Bertram didn't say a word of thanks. He disapproved of the book, he found it frivolous, and since he didn't want to write anything negative, he wrote nothing at all. Very soon after, my husband died. When Bertram sent me his condolences, I wrote back to him, "You probably haven't seen the notice that Fischer put in various newspapers, asking people in possession of letters from Thomas Mann if they'd be kind enough to send them in if they are willing to make them available. In case you have any letters from him that you wouldn't mind having published, it would be nice if you would send them to Fischer. It was like a stroke of fate that we saw you again so soon before my husband's death; he was very happy about it, as you probably were too. When we took leave of one another then, no one could have known that it was to be our last meeting. I'm glad that everything went so smoothly and harmoniously, but to my way of thinking a shadow fell on this reconciliation since you did not see fit to express your thanks for receiving *Krull*—you apparently disapproved of the book, for you didn't even acknowledge it. My husband didn't hold it against you; he said, 'Ach Gott, he doesn't like the book, and since he doesn't want to say so, he won't write anything at all.' But I must say I was very disappointed; it wasn't right."

Bertram never responded to this either. I never heard from him again, and he died fairly soon afterward. Perhaps he was already somewhat feeble and senile; nevertheless I thought he would respond in some way. In earlier days he had had a sense of humor along with all his pedantry. He was a regular German professor. But personally I don't believe that my husband had him in mind when he created the character of Serenus Zeitblom in *Dr. Faustus*.

All the familiar but aged faces after such a long time, after the war! It wasn't always a pleasant experience. We knew Wilhelm Furtwängler, whose father was a very well-known archaeologist when I was a child. He taught at the University of Munich, and my parents knew the family, the way people tend to know one another in academic circles. Willi Furtwängler was perhaps two years younger than we were, my twin brother and I, and at home he was treated like a boy wonder by his mother. He didn't seem to get any older either, simply because he remained the Wunderkind—and then he grew up after all. We met him in Munich from time to time and at Tegernsee, where they had property. Furtwängler stayed in Germany, as the general manager of the Berlin State Opera and conductor of the Philharmonic, whereas we left the country in 1933. When we returned in 1952, he wrote to my husband that it would be nice to get together again. My husband answered that he was honored and pleased, but the barrier between them was too great, and he didn't think a meeting would be productive; perhaps it would be best to let it go. That made Furtwängler terribly angry, and on some occasion or other thereafter he said: "I am not like Thomas Mann, who changes his nationality on every occasion as though it were a shirt." This later appeared in print.

No one thought Thomas Mann would live to be eighty, and least of all that he would remain so productive right up to that age. He was nervous and sensitive and tended to depression, but I suppose most artists are like that. His health was never very stable; there was always something wrong with him. His most severe illness was the lung cancer, from which he recovered so rapidly; not until nine years later did he die of arteriosclerosis. At first, the doctors said it was a thrombosis, but the phlebitis was only a secondary symptom. His lung never caused him any trouble in his remaining years. They had removed one and a half lobes of the right lung and one rib; the other lung, with what remained of the first one, took over all the work. He never suffered from shortness of breath. He did have to make some adjustment in his writing habits; since sitting in his desk chair hurt his back, he exchanged it for the corner of the sofa, where he could rest his arm on its arm, and he held the paper, fastened to a clipboard, on his lap. He kept this arrangement to the end, but otherwise he could move freely and do whatever he wanted.

At the Dutch seaside resort Noordwijk aan Zee, where we went for a vacation during the July of his last year, he could still walk well. The weather remained unusually fine. Every day we went walking by the sea, and when I said, "I think it's time to go back; we have come too far away from the hotel, and we mustn't forget we still have to walk the whole way back," he said, "Oh, let's go a little farther." And one day when the hotel elevator was out of order, he said, "Oh, well, I'll just take the stairs instead." That's how he was almost to the end.

The Schiller year coincided with his eightieth year; for it he wrote his speech ("Essay on Schiller") which he was supposed to deliver on the occasion of the special celebration in Stuttgart. He worked so hard on it that it kept getting longer and longer until it finally grew to one hundred and twenty typewritten pages instead of the twenty pages which had been planned for the address.

Whenever Thomas Mann prepared a lecture, it was too long. Then it was always Erika's task to make the necessary omissions and condensations. She was a master in this. She had to shorten the Schiller address to one-sixth of its written length. This time it was very difficult for her to do. The unabridged essay also appeared as a separate volume.

The ceremony in Stuttgart was impressive. The audience was visibly moved by the address, especially by its conclusion. There is no doubt that it was a great exertion for him. In addition, we went to Lübeck, where we stayed for a week and where he was presented with honorary citizenship. I simply couldn't comprehend how the man could do so much in one day: something in the afternoon, and then in the evening there was a premiere at the theater. I said, "We won't go to that, will we?"

"But of course we're going. It'll be interesting."

On one of the days, he was to give a reading from his own works in the City Theater; he requested that the prelude to *Lohengrin*, which he had listened to with such great enthusiasm as a boy in this very place, be played before the reading; and at the conclusion there was more music. My husband read for an hour and a half, and when it was over, I said to him, "Shall we go now?" for it was evening. He said, "Oh, no. Let's stay with our friends for a while," and then he sat there with them until midnight.

I simply couldn't understand it; I wouldn't have thought him capable of it at all. It was just before his eightieth birthday, and he was so happy about the honorary citizenship and his reconciliation with the city, with *his* city. The head of the city council and the mayor even sent me a lovely telegram for Christmas last year, and I wrote them to express my appreciation and said I knew just how happy my late husband would have been at this kindness—and he would have been.

Yes, Lübeck and its poets! My husband once told me the following story. As a child, he knew the poet Emanuel Geibel, who had been born in Lübeck and, except for one short interlude in Munich, had spent his

entire life there. He went around with his white Van-
dyke beard and a plaid scarf over his shoulder; my husband still remembered seeing him that way. Geibel was
an honorary citizen of the city, and first he received a
lifelong annual pension of several hundred talers from
the Royal Prussian treasury; later he received an additional lifelong pension of 1,000 talers annually from the
king of Prussia (later to be the German Kaiser Wilhelm I). Because he had written such beautiful hymns
to the fatherland during the Franco-Prussian War of
1870–1871, he was also awarded the title "Herald of
the German Reich." When he died, someone told my
husband that an old woman on the street had said, "So
old Geibel is dead. Who's going to get his job now?"
But he was not replaced; the poet laureate had no suc-
cessors. That was the end.

I've already said that Thomas Mann didn't want
to miss going to the theater, even though his visit in
Lübeck was so crowded with other commitments. He
dearly loved the theater, and seeing German drama was
one of the things he especially missed in America. He
himself had written a play in his youth, *Fiorenza*, and
Max Reinhardt—whom he had first known in Berlin
and then got to know better in America—always used
to say to him in Berlin, "Herr Mann, all you have to do
is to write some dialogue, and I'll have it performed immediately, no matter what!" But my husband never
took him up on it. At the very end he wanted to write
another play, *Luther's Wedding*, but he had only

gathered the material, and at his death not a line had been written.

His area was the novel, was prose; he had the feeling of being one of the last great German narrative writers. He was aware that the bourgeois era was over and that something else was coming—and should come —to take its place. But he himself still belonged to his epoch, even though he was inclined to parody its weaknesses.

He wasn't at all sure of posterity's evaluation of his work. He always said, "No one can foresee that." But after all, he has been dead for fifteen years now, and his work continues to live. He always spoke with extraordinary good will of the things that were to come, although their specific contours were indiscernible. He didn't in fact express any regret at the passing of the bourgeois era. Surely he would have mourned the loss of this or that thing which we have witnessed in recent years if he had lived to experience it. He regarded himself personally as one of the last representatives of a great epoch.

Interjections from Outside

E.M.: The Magician has been dead for a long time now, and yet the bridge's span is unbroken, for—and this is very important for us—the fact that our mother is alive and lives among us just as full of life and freshness as she ever was, that she has kept her sense of humor and her drollery intact, as well as her activeness—not only running the house but dominating it (she is truly its mistress)—all this is very important for us and in itself guarantees a continuity which naturally couldn't exist if *she* were no longer there and if all of us had more or less gone our separate ways. We still get together for family celebrations, for Christmas, for birthdays which are getting into the higher numbers for all of us; that creates a strong unbroken continuity too.

G.M.: We have tried to persuade our mother to step more into the limelight; we have attempted this occasionally, but she has always refused. It was a joke among us that she should give a speech on Tolstoy some day. I mean it was a joke that was meant to express what we wished for her. It was always our feeling that she placed her light a little too much under a bushel and that she devoted herself too fully to her tasks, to her manifold duties. Well?

K.M.: I just wanted to say, I have never in my life been able to do what I would have liked to do.

G.M.: No, but after our father's death, you could have come forth a little more, perhaps have written your memoirs or something like that.

K.M.: But I did not want to.

G.M.: There's a book by a French writer on politics, de Moncy, entitled *Les Veuves Abusives*—widows who take advantage of their husbands' fame. She was never cut out to be such a widow, and in my opinion she was a little too unwilling to be one.

K.M.: Psst! Fontane in his old age said, "As long as you live, you have to live," and that's just what I'm trying to do in my way.

Glossary

THEODOR WIESENGRUND-ADORNO (1903–1969): a philosopher, sociologist, and composer. He was an instructor in Frankfurt am Main from 1931 to 1933. In 1934 he emigrated to England, later to the United States. After returning to Germany, he was professor in Frankfurt from 1950 until his death. His works include *Philosophie der neuen Musik* (1949), *Minima moralia* (1951), and *Drei Studien zu Hegel* (1963). See Mann's tribute to him in *The Story of a Novel*, pages 42–48.

HERMANN BAHR (1863–1934): an Austrian critic and playwright. An astute commentator on such modern movements as naturalism and expressionism, Bahr is also remembered for a comedy, *Das Konzert* (*The Concert*, 1909).

RICHARD BEER-HOFMANN (1866–1945): an Austrian playwright and poet who treated Jewish themes in such plays as *Jaakobs Traum* (*Jacob's Dream*, 1918) and *Der junge David* (*Young David*, 1933).

ELSA BERNSTEIN (1866–1949): under the nom de plume of Ernst Rosmer, the author of naturalistic dramas as well as the fairy-tale play *The King's Children* (1895), which Engelbert Humperdinck set to music. She also wrote stories and poems.

MAX BERNSTEIN (1854–1925): married Elsa Bernstein in 1890. A famous lawyer, he was also a prominent theater critic and champion of Ibsen, as well as a writer of comedies for the Munich stage.

Glossary

❀◆❀◆❀◆❀◆❀◆❀◆❀◆❀◆❀◆❀◆❀◆❀

ERNST BERTRAM (1884–1957): a professor of the history of literature; author of *Nietzsche* (1918) and other books.

MAXIMILIAN OSKAR BIRCHER-BENNER (1867–1939): a Swiss doctor who was an early proponent of the importance of natural foods and natural methods of healing in his sanatorium near Zurich.

GEORGE BONDI (1865–1935): a leading Berlin publisher.

FREDERIK BÖÖK: a Stockholm critic and professor of literature who had a voice in the naming of recipients of the Nobel Prize.

GIUSEPPE ANTONIO BORGESE (1882–1952): an Italian writer, historian, and professor of German literature. An anti-fascist, he emigrated to the United States in 1931, and married Elisabeth Mann in 1939. For a time, he taught Italian literature and political science at the University of Chicago. He returned to Italy after the war. Among his works are *Gabriele D'Annunzio* (1909), and in English, *Goliath: The March of Fascism* (1937).

MAX BORN (1882–1970): a physicist who emigrated to England, where he lectured at Cambridge. He became a British subject in 1939. Famed for his research in quantum mechanics, he was awarded the Nobel Prize in 1954.

WOLFGANG BORN (1894–1949): a painter, graphic artist, and illustrator. After emigration to the United States, he taught at Maryville College in St. Louis, and at Queens and City colleges in New York City. His nine colored lithographs for *Death in Venice* were published in Munich as a bibliophilic item in 1921.

PAUL CHARLES JOSEPH BOURGET (1852–1935): a French novelist and critic. He was noted for his psychological studies of modern characters in such works as *Cosmopolis* (1893).

HERMANN BROCH (1886–1951): an Austrian novelist who came to America in 1938 after being briefly imprisoned by the Nazis. Two of his most famous works are *Die Schlaf-wandler* (*The Sleepwalkers*, 1931–1932), which depicts the decline and fall of Wilhelminian Germany from 1880 to 1918, and *Der Tod des Vergil* (*The Death of Virgil*, 1945), an excursion into the past and its myths.

(156)

Glossary

ARNOLT BRONNEN (1895–1959): began as an expressionist dramatist. Though at one time a socialist and friend of Bertolt Brecht, the two parted ways when Bronnen turned to the Nazis.

DR. ERMANNO CECONI: the first husband of the writer Ricarda Huch, whom he married in 1898.

LUDWIG DERLETH (1870–1948): although for a time in contact with the George circle, which published his poems in their periodical *Die Blätter für die Kunst,* he soon set out on independent paths. He emigrated to Switzerland in 1935.

ALFRED DÖBLIN (1878–1957): a novelist and for a long time a practicing neurologist. He was a co-founder in 1910 of the expressionist magazine *Der Sturm.* In 1933 he emigrated to France and in 1940 to the United States. *Berlin Alexanderplatz* (1929), written under the influence of Dos Passos and Joyce, was the most successful of his many novels.

NINON DOLBIN (NÉE AUSLÄNDER): Hermann Hesse's third wife, an art historian, whom he married in 1931.

HEDWIG DOHM (1833–1919): a writer, noted suffragette, and member of a circle that included Franz Liszt and Ferdinand Lassalle.

HANNS EISLER (1898–1962): a composer; disciple of Arnold Schönberg and collaborator of Bertolt Brecht. In 1933 he emigrated by way of Russia to Hollywood, where he wrote music for the films. He returned to East Germany in 1949.

LION FEUCHTWANGER (1884–1958): a novelist and playwright, particularly noted for historical, biographical, and topical novels and revolutionary plays. An erstwhile collaborator of Brecht, he emigrated to the United States in 1940, settling in California.

GOTTFRIED BERMANN FISCHER (b. 1897): M.D., publisher, and son-in-law of S. Fischer. In 1928 he was made manager of S. Fischer Verlag and became head of the firm after the founder's death in 1934. In 1936 he moved the firm to Vienna; from there, after the Anschluss, it was moved

Glossary

❀◈❀◈❀◈❀◈❀◈❀◈❀◈❀◈❀◈❀◈

again to Stockholm. Expelled from Sweden in 1940 for anti-Nazi activity, Fischer moved to the United States, where he helped found L. B. Fischer Corporation. In 1950 he succeeded in reestablishing the venerable firm of S. Fischer Verlag in Frankfurt and Berlin.

SAMUEL FISCHER (1859–1934): the founder and owner of one of Germany's great publishing houses, S. Fischer Verlag. He remained Thomas Mann's publisher and friend throughout his life.

THEODOR FONTANE (1819–1898): a German writer of realistic fiction who turned to the writing of novels quite late in his career. His best, such as *Effi Briest* (1895), portray the morals and manners of Prussian society in his day.

CLEMENS VON FRANCKENSTEIN (1875–1942): a German operatic composer and music conductor.

BRUNO FRANK (1887–1945): a poet, novelist, and playwright. He was Mann's close friend and neighbor, both in Munich and California. Among his works is *Cervantes* (1934).

CHRISTIAN GAUSS (1878–1951): a professor of Romance languages and, from 1925 to 1945, dean of Princeton University.

STEFAN GEORGE (1868–1933): a poet and the center of the George circle, a small group of literary disciples who had a great influence upon German cultural life in the twentieth century. George's poems are marked by frequent obscurity (in the manner of Mallarmé, who was one of his models) and orthographical and typographical innovations.

THERESE GIEHSE (b. 1898): a famous German actress. She created the title role in Brecht's *Mother Courage and Her Children* (1941) and in Dürrenmatt's *The Visit of the Old Lady* (1956), both at the Schauspielhaus in Zurich.

GUSTAF GRÜNDGENS (1899–1963): a famous German actor and theatrical director to whom Erika Mann was briefly married. He was one of the stars of the German stage during the Nazi period.

OLAF GULBRANSSON (1873–1958): a Norwegian artist famed as

(158)

Glossary

❀◇❀◇❀◇❀◇❀◇❀◇❀◇❀◇❀◇❀◇❀

a caricaturist for the satirical Munich periodical *Simplicissimus.*

MARTIN GUMPERT (1897–1955): one of the founders of geriatrics. He was a close friend of the Mann family.

MAX HALBE (1875–1944): a German writer of naturalistic dramas such as *Die Jugend* (*Youth*, 1893).

RICHARD (RICKI) HALLGARTEN: the younger son of Dr. Robert Hallgarten and his wife, Constance. Their house was one of the most cultivated intellectual centers of Munich: Ricki's father was a scholar, philanthropist, and patron of the arts; Frau Hallgarten was a co-founder of the Women's International League for Peace and Freedom. Ricki Hallgarten shot himself in 1932.

MAXIMILIAN HARDEN (1861–1927): a famous Berlin journalist whose revelations of the alleged homosexuality of Prince Eulenburg, a member of Kaiser Wilhelm II's intimate circle, led to the prince's banishment from court as well as to legal action against Harden himself.

EVA HERRMANN (b. 1901): a close friend of the Mann family and a caricaturist whose work has appeared in *The New Yorker* and elsewhere.

PAUL HEYSE (1830–1914): a German novelist and writer of novellas, tremendously popular in his time. He was awarded the Nobel Prize in 1910.

ARTHUR HOLITSCHER (1869–1941): an author of novels and travel books. He and Thomas Mann frequently played music together.

MAX HORKHEIMER (1895–1973): a philosopher and sociologist. A member, along with Theodor W. Adorno and Herbert Marcuse, of the famous Frankfurt school of sociologists. He emigrated to France in 1933 and later to the United States, where he taught at the New School for Social Research. In 1949 he returned to Germany and Frankfurt. His works include *Eclipse of Reason* (1947) and *Studies in Prejudice* (1949).

RICARDA HUCH (1864–1947): a writer and historian; married first to Ermanno Ceconi, then to her cousin Richard Huch. In 1933 she resigned from the Prussian Academy of Arts in protest against National Socialism. She is par-

(159)

ticularly remembered for her writings on German Romanticism.

PAUL HULDSCHINSKY: an interior decorator and film designer; an old friend of the Mann family.

ENGELBERT HUMPERDINCK (1854–1921): a German composer and disciple of Wagner best known for his fairy-tale opera *Hänsel und Gretel* (1893).

ERICH VON KAHLER (1885–1970): a writer, historian, and philosopher. He taught at Princeton University and is the author of *Man the Measure, The Orbit of Thomas Mann,* and *The Inward Turn of Narrative.*

FRANZ KAIM (1856–1935): the founder, in 1893, of the Kaim concerts in Munich, which were especially distinguished under the direction of Felix Weingartner. Kaim's orchestra eventually became the Munich Philharmonic.

FRIEDRICH AUGUST VON KAULBACH (1850–1920): a director of the Munich Academy of Art (1886–1891), famed for his historical canvases and portraits of eminent personalities such as Kaiser Wilhelm II.

GOTTFRIED KELLER (1819–1890): a Swiss-German realist; writer of prose and poetry (including the Swiss national anthem). One of his best-known works is *Die Leute von Seldwyla* (*The People of Seldwyla:* vol. 1, 1856; vol. 2, 1874), a collection of satiric (and occasionally tragic) tales about the inhabitants of a fictional Swiss town.

ALFRED KERR (1867–1948): one of Germany's leading theater critics, famed for his highly subjective and brilliantly written reviews. He emigrated to England in 1933.

HANS KNAPPERTSBUSCH (1888–1965): the conductor and the general music director of the Munich State Opera in 1933.

ANNETTE KOLB (1875–1967): novelist, biographer, essayist, musician. She went into voluntary exile in Paris in 1933 and to the United States in 1940, returning to Paris after the war. Among her works: *Mozart* (1940), *König Ludwig II und Richard Wagner* (1947).

EDUARD KORRODI (1885–1955): a Swiss literary historian and critic. From 1914 to 1950 he was feature editor of the *Neue Zürcher Zeitung.*

Glossary

❧◈❦◈❧◈❦◈❧◈❦◈❧◈❦◈❧◈❦◈❧

FRIEDRICH LANDSHOFF (b. 1901): presently an art publisher in
New York. Between emigrating from Germany and coming to the United States, he worked for the publishing
house of Querido in Amsterdam. He was a close friend
of the Mann family.

ELSE LASKER-SCHÜLER (1876–1945): a poetess and playwright.
She emigrated to Switzerland in 1933 and to Palestine in
1934. Her poems are considered to be among the most
lasting ones connected with the expressionistic movement.

FRANZ VON LENBACH (1836–1904): a fashionable German painter
of the Wilhelminian era.

THEODOR LESSING (1872–1933): a philosopher and mathematician. Lessing was a cultural pessimist whose most popular
work was *Geschichte als Sinngebung des Sinnlosen* (approximately: "History as the Art of Giving Meaning to
Meaninglessness," 1919). He emigrated to Czechoslovakia
in 1933, where he was murdered by Nazi agents.

MAKSIM LITVINOV (1876–1951): a Soviet diplomat and commis-
sar for foreign affairs. He was ambassador to the United
States from November 1941 to August 1943. In August
1946 he retired from public life.

HENDRIK WILLEM VAN LOON (1882–1944): a Dutch-born
American journalist and historian who had a popular
success with such works as *The Story of Mankind* (1921)
and *Van Loon's Lives* (1942).

SAMUEL LUBLINSKI (1868–1910): the first critic to point out, in
a review in *Das Berliner Tageblatt*, the lasting signifi-
cance of *Buddenbrooks* when it appeared in 1901. The
author of a four-volume study, *Literature and Society in
the Nineteenth Century*, which appeared in 1899, he also
wrote historical dramas such as *Peter of Russia* (1906).

GEORG LUKÁCS (1885–1971): a Hungarian Marxist philosopher
and literary historian. He was a member of the Communist Party from 1918 on, although he found himself in
official disfavor from time to time for not adhering closely
enough to the program for socialist realism in literature.
His book on Mann has appeared in English as *Essays on
Thomas Mann* (1965).

ALMA MAHLER-WERFEL (1879–1964): the wife successively of

(161)

Glossary

❀✿❀✿❀✿❀✿❀✿❀✿❀✿❀✿❀✿❀✿❀✿❀✿❀

Walter Gropius, Gustav Mahler, and Franz Werfel. She is the author of *Gustav Mahler* (1939) and of an autobiography, *And the Bridge Is Love* (1958).

NELLY KRÖGER MANN: Heinrich Mann's second wife, whom he married in 1939.

JULIUS MEIER-GRAEFE (1867–1935): a noted art historian. He prepared the ground for impressionism in Germany.

FELIX MOTTL (1856–1911): an Austrian composer and conductor, especially famed for his performances of Wagner; at one time, director of the Royal Opera in Munich.

ROBERT MUSIL (1880–1942): an Austrian novelist who emigrated to Switzerland in 1938. His literary debut was the school novel *Die Verwirrungen des Zöglings Törless* (*The Confusions of Young Törless*, 1906). His vast magnum opus, *Der Mann ohne Eigenschaften* (*The Man Without Qualities*, 1930–1942), was never completed but has won increasing recognition since World War II.

CAROLINE NEWTON (1893–1975): daughter of the noted American bibliophile A. Edward Newton, a book collector in her own right, and a benefactor of libraries.

LUIGI NONO (b. 1924): an Italian composer who adopted Schönberg's twelve-tone system in his own works, such as the *Variazioni canoniche* for orchestra (1950).

HANS PFITZNER (1869–1949): a late Romantic composer. His *Palestrina*, first performed by Bruno Walter in Munich in 1917, made a deeper impression on Thomas Mann than any opera since he had first heard Wagner.

JOSEF PONTEN (1883–1940): a novelist whose chief work was *Volk auf dem Wege: Roman der deutschen Unruhe* (*People on Their Way: A Novel of German Restlessness*, 1934–1942), five volumes, unfinished.

EMIL PREETORIUS (1883–1973): a former president of the Bavarian Academy of Fine Arts in Munich, stage designer, artist, writer, book designer, collector of Asiatic art. He was responsible for epoch-making reforms in the presentation of Wagnerian operas.

HERMANN REIFF (1856–1938): a silk manufacturer, married to Lilly Sertorius (1866–1958). The Reiffs, art-loving, hos-

(162)

Glossary

✿◇✿◇✿◇✿◇✿◇✿◇✿◇✿◇✿◇✿◇✿◇✿◇✿

pitable, patrons of the arts, played a unique part in Zurich society: Swiss and foreign musicians, actors, writers, and painters would mingle at the Reiff home with diplomats, gentleman farmers, manufacturers, and princes.

COUNTESS FRANZISKA ZU REVENTLOW (1871–1918): a novelist who was both a member and chronicler of the Bohemian life in Munich's Schwabing at the turn of the century.

PAUL RILLA (1896–1954): a literary and theater critic. After World War II, he was one of the editors of the *Berliner Zeitung* (East Berlin).

WALTER RILLA (b. 1894): until 1933 a film actor, principally in Berlin. During the war he emigrated to London. Since 1955 he has appeared again on the German stage (especially on television).

WILHELM CONRAD RÖNTGEN (1845–1923): German physicist and discoverer of X-rays.

RENÉ SCHICKELE (1883–1940): a novelist, poet, and playwright. An Alsatian with a German father and French mother, Schickele wrote in German. He edited the pacifist, expressionist journal *Die weissen Blätter* (*The White Pages*) in Zurich during World War I. In 1933 he voluntarily emigrated to France, where he died. Among his works: *Das Erbe am Rhein* (*Heritage on the Rhine*, 1925–1931), a novel in three volumes. Long acquainted with Thomas Mann, Schickele became a close friend from 1933 on.

MAX VON SCHILLINGS (1868–1933): a composer and opera conductor, much influenced by Wagner. His chief work is the opera *Mona Lisa* (1915).

ARTHUR SCHNITZLER (1862–1931): an Austrian novelist and playwright who portrayed the lives and loves of the Viennese in such works as *Anatol* (1891) and *Reigen* (*La Ronde*, 1900). His schooling in medicine (especially in psychiatry) is generally held responsible for the probing view he takes of his characters, especially of their unconscious motivations.

KLAUS SCHRÖTER: a Germanist and the author of *Thomas Mann in Selbstzeugnissen und Bilddokumenten* (*Thomas Mann in His Own Words* [*Illustrated*], 1964). Schröter's doctoral dissertation at the University of Hamburg (1960) concerned the literary influences upon the young Heinrich Mann.

MOLLY SHENSTONE: the wife of Allen Shenstone, who was a professor of physics at Princeton during World War II.

HERMANN STEHR (1864–1940): a naturalist author of novels about the Silesian peasantry which were extremely popular with the Nazis.

WILHELM EMANUEL SÜSKIND (1901–1970): a German novelist and journalist. After the war he wrote a book on the Nürnberg trials and, from 1949 on, was editor of the influential *Süddeutsche Zeitung* in Munich.

HENRI TEMIANKA (b. 1906): an internationally known American violinist; conductor of the Temianka Little Symphony Orchestra (1956–1960).

BERTHOLD VIERTEL (1885–1953): an Austrian writer and theatrical director. He directed the American premiere of Brecht's *The Private Life of the Master Race*. After the war he returned to his native Vienna, where he was active at the famous Burgtheater.

HELENE WEIGEL (1900–1971): an eminent actress and the wife of Bertolt Brecht. After his death, she became the director of his famous Berliner Ensemble.

FELIX WEINGARTNER (1863–1942): a conductor and composer. Successor of Gustav Mahler at the Vienna Court Opera (1908–1911); later, director of the Vienna State Opera (1934–1936).

FRANZ WERFEL (1890–1945): an Austrian novelist, poet, and playwright, born in Prague. In his early years an expressionist with a mystical-religious bent, Werfel later won worldwide fame with such novels as *Die vierzig Tage von Musa Dagh* (*The Forty Days of Musa Dagh*, 1933) and *Das Lied von Bernadette* (*The Song of Bernadette*, 1941). He fled the Nazis, coming to the United States in 1940. He died in California.

WITTELSBACH: a German dynasty whose members were rulers of Bavaria and the Rhenish Palatinate until this century.

KARL WOLFSKEHL (1869–1948): a poet and member of Stefan

(164)